# LIES
## *Women*
# BELIEVE

### STUDY GUIDE

# LIES
## *Women*
# BELIEVE

---

### STUDY GUIDE

---

# NANCY DeMOSS
# WOLGEMUTH

**MOODY PUBLISHERS**

CHICAGO

This is a revised edition of *The Companion Guide for Lies Women Believe* (© 2002).

Edited by Anne C. Buchanan
Interior design: Puckett Smartt
Cover concept: Amjad Shahzad
Cover design: Erik M. Peterson
Cover images: Front cover photo of apple with bite copyright © 2014 by eli_asenova/iStock (475190475). All rights reserved. Back cover illustration of apple tree copyright © 2014 by WesAbrams/iStock (487774771). All rights reserved.
Author photo: Nathan Bollinger

Library of Congress Cataloging-in-Publication Data

Names: Wolgemuth, Nancy DeMoss, author.
Title: Lies women believe : study guide ; a life-changing resource for individuals and groups / Nancy DeMoss Wolgemuth.
Description: CHICAGO : MOODY PUBLISHERS, 2018. | Includes bibliographical references.
Identifiers: LCCN 2017054982 (print) | LCCN 2018006377 (ebook) | ISBN 9780802495167 () | ISBN 9780802414984
Subjects: LCSH: Christian women--Religious life--Textbooks. | Truthfulness and falsehood--Religious aspects--Christianity--Textbooks.
Classification: LCC BV4527 (ebook) | LCC BV4527 .D46155 2018 (print) | DDC 248.8/43071--dc23
LC record available at https://lccn.loc.gov/2017054982

ISBN 13: 978-0-8024-1498-4

We hope you enjoy this book from Moody Publishers. Our goal is to provide high-quality, thought-provoking books and products that connect truth to your real needs and challenges. For more information on other books and products written and produced from a biblical perspective, go to www.moodypublishers.com or write to:

Moody Publishers
820 N. LaSalle Boulevard
Chicago, IL 60610

5 7 9 10 8 6 4

*Printed in the United States of America*

*S*ince the original release of *Lies Women Believe*, we have received many encouraging responses from women describing the impact this message is having on their thinking and their walk with God. Women of every age, in every season of life, have had their eyes opened to the lies they have believed and have been set free by the Truth. One woman, a long-time friend, wrote the following:

> I cannot tell you the depth of work God is doing. Frankly, I am appalled at what lies
> I have allowed to permeate my thinking and subsequently have become my lifestyle.
> The thing that is so thrilling is to finally be able to identify those lies and to discover
> what hope there is in the Truth of God's Word to deliver me from the lies.

Many women are finally "connecting the dots"—realizing how deception in one area has consequences in other areas of their lives, as illustrated by this testimony:

> As I approach sixty years of age, I have seen that episodes of "depression" and long-
> standing struggles with anxiety are rooted in my misunderstandings about the character
> and nature of God.

Some have shared honestly that it was not an easy book to read. One woman phrased it this way: "It was like having a 'spiritual root canal'—only on my *heart*." Now, that's not the kind of testimonial that generally motivates people to read a book! However, she went on to express the blessing she is experiencing as a result of walking through the pain:

> I am learning to cherish the Word. There is such great joy in drinking deeply of it;
> it satisfies my longings, cleanses my mind, and leaves me craving more!

I have been especially glad to learn of women who are meeting together in small group settings to read and discuss the book. Again, the reports have been so encouraging. One woman told us that in her group "women are opening up and revealing lies they didn't even realize were lies and are able to face the lies with God's Truth."

This study guide has been designed to help women who want to go deeper in understanding and applying the message of *Lies Women Believe* (updated and expanded version, 2018)—either individually or with a group. If possible, I would encourage you to do this study with others—whether a small group or simply one or two other women who want to grow in their walk with God. A group setting will provide encouragement and accountability as you grapple with various lies you or others may have believed, and as you seek to root out those lies and begin to walk in the Truth.

Throughout the course of this study, as you read, reflect, and respond, I pray you will open your heart to the Lord and ask Him to show you where you may have been subtly deceived. Then trust Him to show you how to walk in the Truth and how to point others to the Truth that can set them free.

No matter how challenging or difficult the walk may prove to be at points, He has promised to walk with you. He will be your Companion, Guide, Helper, and Friend all the way till the end of the journey and then through all eternity!

Nancy DeMoss Wolgemuth
February 2018

This guide is designed to be a companion study to the book *Lies Women Believe*. You'll need to have a copy of the book in order to follow along in the study. (Note: Be sure you're using the 2018 updated and expanded edition of *Lies*, as this *Study Guide* is keyed to that version.) You will be assigned a few pages in the book to read along with each day's study. Each week in this study includes the following features:

- **IN A NUTSHELL**—An introductory section that gives you an overview of the chapter and the lies discussed in that chapter.

- **EXPLORING THE TRUTH**—Five days of personal study to complete before your small group meeting. These lessons are designed to help you think through how to incorporate God's Truth in your daily life. Each day's study includes Scriptures to meditate on and questions to answer under the subtitles "Realize," "Reflect," and "Respond."

- **WALKING TOGETHER IN THE TRUTH**—Questions to be discussed when your small group meets. If you are not doing this as part of a group study, you can use this section as an extra day or two of personal study. The questions are different from what you'll find in the other lessons and will challenge you with further application of the Truth.

Don't be in a hurry as you work through the questions. They are meant to encourage you to think through your attitudes and beliefs. You may find it difficult to respond honestly to some of them. Wrestling with those areas is an important part of the process and will help you grow. As the Spirit works in your heart, keep opening it up to Him, asking what He wants to teach you. If you miss a day, don't give up! Bible study is a discipline, but it yields sweet fruit for those who are willing to pay the price.

May the Lord make Himself known to you as you seek Him in His Word, and may you experience the freedom and joy of walking in the Truth.

# CHAPTER ONE

# LAYING THE *Foundation*

## IN A NUTSHELL . . .

The introduction, prologue, and chapter 1 of *Lies Women Believe* lay a foundation for understanding the power of Satan's lies in our culture and in our personal lives, and for discovering the powerful Truth found in God's Word.

Jesus came to give us abundant life. So why do we sometimes find ourselves living defeated, lonely, fearful, stressed-out lives? The problem is that we've believed a lie—or lies—from Satan's arsenal. Not all of them, of course. In fact, we might be tempted to pride ourselves on not believing the Enemy. But there may be just one little lie hanging like a luscious piece of fruit that we have picked and eaten. Perhaps we didn't see that it was a lie. It looked so innocent, even helpful. Or perhaps it was so tempting that we just couldn't resist. In any case, we've discovered that even one "simple" lie can place us in bondage and keep us from experiencing the joyous, confident, peaceful life Christ offers.

If you're experiencing bondage in any area of your life, I pray that this book will help you identify any lies you may have believed and the corresponding Truth from God's Word. I hope you will come to see that none of Satan's lies *are* harmless. We can't give in to them and come away unaffected. We need to learn to discern those lies when we encounter them, to <u>replace the lies with the Truth</u>, and then to help others do the same.

> NOTE FROM *Nancy*
>
> *"I'm not talking about a magic formula that will make problems vanish; I'm not offering any shortcuts to an easy life, nor am I promising the absence of pain and difficulties. Life is hard— there's no way around that. But I am talking about walking through the realities of life— things like rejection, loss, disappointment, wounds, and even death—in freedom and true joy." (pp. 18–19)*

# THE POWER OF THE TRUTH *(pp. 15–24)\**
## DAY ONE

### REALIZE

1. Read John 10:10. As you think about your life, would you say you are experiencing the abundant life Jesus came to give? Or do you find yourself just coping, surviving, or struggling along? Explain.

   _____

   _____

### REFLECT

2. Look at the list of words on page 16 of *Lies Women Believe*. List below any of those words that describe your current season of life. Add other words of your own if needed. (If you are not currently dealing with these kinds of feelings but you know someone who is, describe how you think she is feeling. You can use this study to learn how to help her and others who are struggling.)

   _____

   _____

3. Look at the list of words on page 18 of *Lies Women Believe*. Write below the words (or any of your own) that you would like to describe your life.

   _____

   _____

4. Read John 8:31–36. What do you think Jesus meant when He talked about being free? How do you know He did not mean being free to do anything we want to do?

   _____

   _____

5. Read Galatians 5:1 and John 14:6. What (Who) is the Truth that sets us free?

   _____

   _____

*\*Unless otherwise indicated, page numbers correspond to pages in *Lies Women Believe* (updated and expanded version, 2018).*

## RESPOND

6. The woman whose story begins on page 21 said she had "given up hope" that she could ever be completely free from the moral habit that had kept her in bondage for years. Is there any area of your life where you have given up hope that you can be set free?

_____

_____

7. How would you like for your life to change as a result of this study?

_____

_____

*Lord, I want to grow through this study. I pray that You will show me any areas where I'm in bondage and reveal any lies I've believed that are holding me there. Show me the Truth I need to know so I can be truly free. Amen.*

# KNOWING YOUR ENEMY *(pp. 27–32)*
## DAY TWO

## REALIZE

1. What do the following verses tell you about Satan and the way he operates?
   John 8:44

_____

_____

   2 Corinthians 4:4

_____

_____

   2 Corinthians 11:14

_____

_____

   Ephesians 6:11–12

_____

_____

1 Peter 5:8

_____

_____

2. Which of these characteristics do you see in the Genesis 3 account of Satan's temptation of Eve?

_____

_____

NOTE FROM *Nancy*

*"Regardless of the immediate source, anytime we receive input that is not consistent with the Word of God, our antennae should go up. What we read or hear may sound right, may feel right, may seem right—but if it's contrary to the Word of God, it isn't right."* (p. 32)

### REFLECT

3. Why do Satan's lies often appear good and attractive?

_____

_____

_____

4. What are some of the forms Satan's deception takes in our culture?

_____

_____

_____

5. How can you discern the difference between Truth and deception? How can you keep from being deceived by Satan's lies?

_____

_____

_____

### RESPOND

6. We will be more vulnerable to deception if we're not regularly meditating on God's Word. What "good" things can keep you away from consistent study of the Word?

_____

_____

7. How can you raise your awareness of the Enemy and his attempts to deceive you?

_____

_____

*Lord, I know that Satan is a real enemy and that he would like to make me ineffective for You and Your kingdom. Help me to stay in Your Word and to remember that no matter how powerful Satan may be, You are infinitely more powerful! Amen.*

# OPENING YOUR EYES *(pp. 32–37)*
## DAY THREE

## REALIZE

1. Read Genesis 2:15–17 and 3:1–13. What seemingly good thing did Satan offer to Eve? Why did she think it was a good offer?

_____

_____

## REFLECT

2. Make a list of the primary sources of input you have coming into your life (e.g., movies, books, friends, social media, a counselor).

_____

_____

_____

3. How careful are you about evaluating that input and seeking to discern Truth from error? Check the statement below that best describes you:

☐ I have been heavily influenced by the culture and other "voices" around me and don't generally stop to evaluate what I hear and see in light of God's Word. I am not discerning when it comes to Truth and error. (If this is true, you may not even realize that it describes you!)

☐ I am careful in some areas but not in others. I need to grow in spiritual discernment.

☐ I evaluate the things I hear and see through the grid of God's Word and carefully consider the consequences when tempted with wrong choices. (According to Hebrews 5:14, the ability to discern between good and evil is a mark of spiritual maturity.)

> NOTE FROM *Nancy*
>
> *"It's tempting to mindlessly accept whatever we hear and see. . . . How often do we make choices without stopping to consider the consequences that may follow? Many of us simply live our lives, responding to the people, circumstances, and influences around us. . . . It all looks so good; it feels so right; it seems so innocent. But we end up in abusive relationships, head over heels in debt, angry, frustrated, trapped, and overwhelmed. We have been deceived."*
> *(pp. 35–36)*

4. Describe a time when you made a wrong choice without stopping to consider the cost and the consequences.

_____

_____

5. Identify the lie that Satan used to lead you to believe that you (or others) would not be affected by the sin.

_____

_____

6. What truth from God's Word could have helped you walk away from Satan's lie?

_____

_____

## RESPOND

7. Ask God to help you grow in your ability to discern good from evil and to make godly choices. Ask Him to show you if there is any area of your life where you are currently being deceived by input that is contrary to the Word of God.

*Father, open my eyes so I won't be deceived by Satan's lies.*
*Sometimes a course of action seems right when I don't stop to think about Your Truth or about the*
*consequences that could result. Teach me to consider my choices in light of Your Word. Amen.*

# SEEING THE PROGRESSION *(pp. 37–40)*
## DAY FOUR

## REALIZE

1. From pages 37–39 in *Lies Women Believe*, what are the four steps that take us from initial deception to bondage?

   1. _____

   2. _____

   3. _____

   4. _____

2. Look again at Genesis 3:1–13. What did Eve do that matched each of these four steps that led her from deception to bondage?

    1. _____

       _____

    2. _____

       _____

    3. _____

       _____

    4. _____

       _____

## REFLECT

3. As long as we live in this world, we can't completely isolate ourselves so that we never hear any lies. What's the difference between "hearing" lies and "listening to" them?

   _____

   _____

4. Read Philippians 4:8–9. Why is it so important to be selective about the input we allow to come into our minds and to choose to expose ourselves and listen to the Truth?

   _____

   _____

> NOTE FROM *Nancy*
>
> *"There are no harmless lies. We cannot expose ourselves to the world's false, deceptive way of thinking and come out unscathed." (p. 38)*

## RESPOND

5. Review the list you made on Day Three—the sources of input that you allow to come into your life. Is there anything on that list that is exposing you unnecessarily to deception?

   _____

   _____

6. What steps can you take to better protect your mind and heart from Satan's deception?

   _____

   _____

*Lord, please show me any ways that I have made myself more vulnerable
to Satan's lies by the kinds of influences I choose to allow into my life.
Help me to fill my mind and heart with the Truth. Amen.*

# CLAIMING THE TRUTH *(pp. 40–43)*
### DAY FIVE

## REALIZE

1. What are the three steps that will help us move from spiritual bondage to freedom?

   1. _____

   2. _____

   3. _____

> ### NOTE FROM *Nancy*
>
> *"Satan is a formidable enemy. His primary weapon is deception. His lies are powerful. But there is something even more powerful than Satan's lies—and that is the Truth." (p. 41)*

## REFLECT

2. How does the Truth counter lies?

   _____

   _____

3. What does the Bible say about Truth in the following verses?

   Psalm 33:4 _____

   Psalm 51:6 _____

   John 8:32 _____

   John 17:17 _____

   2 Timothy 2:15 _____

4. Read John 14:15–17 and 16:13. What is the Holy Spirit's role in helping us discern and walk in the Truth?

   _____

   _____

## RESPOND

5. Can you identify any specific area(s) of bondage in your life—areas where you are not walking in freedom? (See pages 40–41 in *Lies Women Believe* for examples of common types of bondage.)

   _____

   _____

   _____

6. "Every area of bondage in our lives can be traced back to a lie" (p. 40). Ask God to help you during the course of this study to discover what lie(s) you have believed that may have placed you in bondage. Also ask the Lord to show you the Truth from His Word that counters Satan's lies.

*Lord, I pray that You will show me clearly any lies I have believed.*
*Then show me the Truth that will set me free. Thank You for Your Word and for Your Holy Spirit,*
*which point me to the Truth. Help me to walk in Your Truth today and every day. Amen.*

## WALKING TOGETHER IN THE TRUTH . . .

1. Why is our understanding of Truth ⌐Jesus so important?

   The impetus between a holy life
   or a sinful life; anxiety, addiction,
   selfishness
   The truth will set you free

2. A popular theme in our culture is that there are no absolutes. "All truth is good. Whatever truth works for you is good for you, and what works for me is good for me." While on the surface that appears quite tolerant, where does this kind of thinking ultimately lead?

   death
   tossed about by every wave

> ### NOTE FROM *Nancy*
>
> "From that first encounter in the garden to the present day, Satan has used deception to win our affections, influence our choices, and destroy our lives. In one way or another, every problem we have in this world is the fruit of deception— the result of believing something that simply isn't true." (p. 32)

3. Describe some lies that are widely accepted as Truth by our society. What are some ways these lies influence people's choices, and how can they be destructive?

   Follow your heart; you are good enough; = self idolatry
   deceitful above all else

4. List three or four widespread problems in our world and discuss how each could be the result of deception.
   - LGBTQ — identity; worth or appetite          No absolute truth
   - Human Trafficking — devalue God's creation
   - Climate change Agenda — man centric

5. Can you think of any women in the Scripture who were
   deceived and who then influenced others to sin? (Need some
   help? Take a look at Genesis 3:6 and 16:1–6.)

   *daughters of Lots    Miriam*
   *Sarah *              *Jezebel*

6. Discuss some ways women in our day have been deceived. How
   has that deception influenced their own choices and the choices
   of others?

   *Hillary Clinton    Madonna*
   *Feminism ; sexual liberation*
   *You can have it all.        abortion*
   *a snake eating it tail*

7. Share one or more ways that you have opened yourself up to deception in the past by choosing
   to expose yourself to input that is contrary to the Truth.

   *T.V. sitcoms ; music ; books, anime*

8. What are some illustrations of Satan's offers that women today find appealing? (Keep in mind
   that the things Satan tempts us with are not always inherently evil. The fruit that Eve ate
   wasn't bad or sinful in and of itself—in fact, it was something God had created. What made
   Eve's choice sinful was that God had said not to eat the fruit.)

   *fame & attention ; power ; freedom ; materialism*

9. Share a choice you were tempted to make that looked appealing
   and seemed right but was contrary to God's Word. If you fell for
   the lie, describe any negative consequences that resulted.

   *gossiping with friends*

10. Read together Acts 17:10–12. What did the people in Berea do
    in order to discern the Truth? How can we avoid being deceived
    and become more discerning about the input we receive?

    *dug into the word*

    *Job 23:13*
    *treasured His words more than*
    *my daily bread.*

# CHAPTER TWO

# TRUSTING *God*

## IN A NUTSHELL . . .

C hapter 2 discusses six lies that many women wrestle with as they work through their view of God. This is important because what we believe about God affects our outlook on everything else.

The first lie focuses on questioning God's goodness. The Bible tells us that God is good. However, in a world filled with hatred and evil, it is tempting to question His goodness. Even if we know in our minds that God is good, our personal circumstances might lead us to doubt that He is good to us. In either case, our doubt can make us prone to discouragement and bitterness and lead us to justify disobeying God's Word. Walking in the Truth means acknowledging that God is completely good and that everything He does is good. Yes, human sin has given birth to enormous evil in the world. But God is powerful enough to bring good results even out of evil circumstances.

The second lie concerns God's love. Many women don't believe that God could possibly love them. Though they may intellectually know of God's love, their feelings contradict what they know. They don't *feel* loved, so they don't believe that they are loved. To avoid falling for that lie, we need to move beyond our feelings and focus on the fact of God's love for us—a love so intense that He gave His Son to die for us.

The third lie addresses a major hurdle for many women. They cannot envision God as their loving Father because their earthly fathers were unloving—demanding, abusive, absent, or critical. These women need to understand that God is not like any human they have ever known. He is perfect and perfectly good and loving.

The fourth lie is one we are all tempted to believe, if not consciously, then in actuality. It is the lie that God is not enough—that we must have some thing(s) in addition to Him, in order to be complete, happy, and fulfilled. In reality, though, when we have God, we have all we really need for our peace, joy, and satisfaction.

Fifth is the lie that if we live God's way, we will be miserable. Many people think of God's commands as a burden rather than a blessing. The Bible makes clear, however, that Jesus came to set people free. The Bible gives guidance and instruction that protect and bless us when we obey—and we disobey at our own peril. True freedom and joy are found in obedience.

Finally, a sixth lie that many women believe about God is that He should fix all their problems—here and now—that they should enjoy problem-free lives. But God never promised to make life easy. He does promise to walk through life with us, using the problems that come our way to mold us and shape us into the image of His Son.

## EXPLORING THE TRUTH . . .

# GOD IS GOOD *(pp. 47–51)*
## DAY ONE

### REALIZE

1. When you were a child, you may have prayed this little rhyme before meals: "God is great, God is good . . . " Suppose you had never been to church and had never read a Bible. Would you think that a good God exists? Why or why not?

   *Yes b/c stars & warm days & flowers & grandma cookies*

---

NOTE FROM *Nancy*

*"Theologically, intellectually, we know that God is good. But deep in many of our hearts, there lurks a suspicion that He may not really be good—at least, that He has not been good to us." (p. 49)*

---

2. Look up Ephesians 1:3–14. List several blessings mentioned in this passage that you are particularly grateful for.

   *Saved young v 5*
   *the deposit of the H.S. v. 13*
   *forgiveness v 7*

3. According to Psalms 34:8 and 106:1, what are appropriate responses to the goodness of God?

   *Taste & See (try Him out)*
   *Praise & thanks*

## REFLECT

1. Describe a situation, either past or present, in which you have been tempted to question God's goodness. (For example, difficult marriage, an unanswered prayer, an unexpected illness...)

*No husband, no career, no children*

5. Romans 8:28 is a familiar verse to many believers. Read that verse as well as verses 29–39. What perspective about God and His good purposes does this passage provide to help us face painful or difficult life situations?

*according to His purpose v. 28     trials cannot*
*conformed to the image of His Son v. 29   undo Gods purposes*
*for us.*

## RESPOND

6. Psalm 118:1 exhorts us to "give thanks to the Lord, for he is good." Talk to God about a difficult situation you are facing. Thank Him for His goodness, and claim the promise of Romans 8:28–29. Here's a sample prayer: "Lord, even though I am in a hard place regarding _____, I know You are good and You have promised to work that situation out for good. I know Your commitment is to make me like Jesus. Thank You that You will use this circumstance (or person) as a means to fulfill Your good purpose for my life."

*Lord, I know You are good, but deep down I sometimes wonder about Your goodness when I'm facing hard times. Help me to trust in Your goodness, even when I cannot see it clearly. Amen.*

# GOD IS LOVING (pp. 52–56)
## DAY TWO

## REALIZE

1. Based on John 15:13, how did Jesus show His love for you? What else does the Bible tell you about God's love? (See John 3:16, Romans 5:8, 1 John 4:7–10.)

*laid down his life,  Father gave the Son,  He loved us first*
*for sinners ,*

2. What effect do your feelings have on the Truth of God's love for you?

*None! I am a liar w/ a deceitful heart - Why would I listen? God's love for me is not affected by me.*

**REFLECT**

3. Even though you may know that God loves you, you may not always feel that He does. What are some of the things that can cause you to feel that no one really loves or cares about you?

*Criticism, pride of life*

4. How can you live within the reality of God's love even on those days when you don't feel His love?

*Songs, gratitude, prayer discipline to shut down neg. thoughts*

**RESPOND**

5. How might our lives be different if we could fully grasp the greatness of God's love? How would you think differently about God, about yourself, and about your circumstances if you truly understood how much God loves you?

*Fearless; greater grace towards others! Joyfull (in all things)*

6. How can you grow in your understanding of the love of God?

*Scripture read to better understand God's character (Bible Recap)*

7. Read Paul's prayer in Ephesians 3:14–19. Personalize this prayer and pray it for yourself or for someone you know who has difficulty accepting the love of God.

*That I, being rooted and grounded in love [Jesus], may be able to comprehend with all the Saints the breadth, length, depth and height; to know the love of Christ which passes knowledge.*

Lord, I know that You love me. But I admit that on some days, I just don't feel it.

Remind me at those times not to trust my feelings

but to believe the Truth You have revealed in Your Word. Amen.

# GOD IS ENOUGH *(pp. 56–57)*

## DAY THREE

## REALIZE

1. Take a look at some ads and commercials currently running on TV, the internet, or in magazines. What are some things they tell us we need in order to be truly fulfilled, happy, and complete?

   *makeup, hair, vacation*

2. Read Colossians 2:9–10. What does it mean that you have been given "fullness" or "completeness" in Christ?

   *All that we need (theologically, philosophically concerning our soul & intellect) is provided in Christ*

## REFLECT

3. Do you really believe that if you have God, you have enough? What are some of the "pluses" you tend to think you need in order to be happy?

   *job, money, helpmate, children, nice house*
   *ability to shop, go places (take trips)*

4. What are some <u>practical ways</u> we can wean ourselves from dependence on earthly, temporal things and find greater satisfaction in Christ?

   *Praise Him then ask*
   *Discipline of self denial*
   *Gratitude!*

## RESPOND

5. Read Psalm 73:23–26. Personalize Asaph's prayer and write it in your own words. Ask God to make this prayer the true expression of your heart.

   _____

   _____

   _____

   _____

> ### NOTE FROM *Nancy*
>
> "Do you truly believe God is enough, or do you find yourself turning to other things and people—food, shopping, friends, hobbies, vacations, job, family—to fill the empty places of your heart?" (p. 56)

*Father, I'm prone to look to people and things other than You to fill the empty places of my heart and to satisfy my needs and longings. Your Word tells me that when I have You, I am complete. Thank You that no matter what else I may or may not have in this life, with You I have enough. Amen.*

# THE LAW OF LIBERTY *(pp. 57–60)*
## DAY FOUR

### REALIZE

1. What would the world be like if there were no laws? In what ways are laws necessary and beneficial to a society?

   _____

   _____

2. What does Deuteronomy 6:24–25 say about the value and blessing of obedience to God's laws?

   _____

   _____

NOTE FROM *Nancy*

*"The Scripture teaches that God's laws are for our good. Obedience is the pathway to freedom. But Satan places in our minds the idea that God's laws are burdensome, unreasonable, and unfair and that if we obey Him we'll be miserable."* (p. 57)

### REFLECT

3. Read James 1:19–27. What does James mean when he refers to "the perfect law, the law of liberty" (v. 25)? How do God's laws give us freedom?

   _____

   _____

   _____

   _____

4. Describe a time when you decided to do your own thing instead of obeying God. What happened?

   _____

   _____

   _____

   _____

5. In what ways are God's restrictions actually a benefit and a blessing to His children? How could you explain their benefit to others?

_____

_____

## RESPOND

6. Are there any biblical commands you have been resisting or hesitating to obey, thinking you would be better off doing things your way? What are they? Keeping in mind that "obedience is the pathway to freedom" (p. 57), what would it take for you to surrender and choose to obey?

> *Lord, I know that the direction in Your Word has been given to us out of love.*
> *Help me to trust You and to be willing to obey You*
> *even when Your ways do not make sense to my finite mind. Amen.*

# DIVINE DELAYS AND DENIALS *(pp. 60–62)*
## DAY FIVE

### REALIZE

1. What are some illustrations of the way our society is conditioned to expect quick fixes?

_____

_____

2. Read 2 Corinthians 12:7–10. What kind of problem does Paul describe in this passage? What do you think his motivation was in asking for it to be removed? Do you think he was wrong to pray this way?

_____

_____

3. What was God's response to Paul's request?

_____

_____

NOTE FROM *Nancy*

*"The Truth is, life is hard. We live in a fallen world. Even those who have been redeemed live in earthly bodies and have to deal with the realities of temptation, sin (both our own and others'), disease, loss, pain, and death. . . . God is not removed or detached from our problems. . . . He uses pressures and problems to mold and shape our lives and to make us like His Son, Jesus." (p. 61)*

## REFLECT

4. Are there problems and trials in your life that you've asked God to remove and He has not?

_____

_____

_____

_____

5. Why might God choose not to fix or remove certain problems? What greater goals might He have in mind? If God chooses not to remove your difficulties, what might He be trying to do instead? (See Job 23:10, Romans 5:3–4, James 1:2–4.)

_____

_____

_____

_____

_____

6. In what ways have you seen God work through difficulties in your life or in others' lives?

_____

_____

_____

## RESPOND

7. Identify the biggest problem you are facing currently. What might God want to teach you through this struggle? If God never "fixed" that problem, how could He use this circumstance to change you and to reveal His character through you?

_____

_____

_____

*Lord, I know You want what is best for me. You desire to help me become mature.
I understand that sometimes the only way I will grow is through pain. In the difficulties
I'm facing today, please grant me peace and patience to accept
Your perfect will in my life. Amen.*

## WALKING TOGETHER IN THE TRUTH . . .

1. Why does our view of God matter so much?

   *Nucleus of faith; prime reason of religion*

   *"God shot" Tara Lee Cobb*

2. What are some faulty views people have of God? How do those views affect the way people live?

   *Clockmaker, Genie, not Good, powerless not involved*

3. In your reading and study of chapter 2, what Truth about God did you find particularly encouraging or helpful? (See pages 63–64 in *Lies Women Believe*.)

   *2 Cor 4:17    Col. 3:4 – Christ, who is our life light affliction, but for a moment    Romans 8:28–39 ! Who condemns you, it is Christ who died.*

■ **LIE #1: God is not really good.**

■ **TRUTH:** God is good, and everything He does is good. He never makes mistakes.

4. What is the source of evil in the world? Read Genesis 3:1–8 and discuss how sin has affected all people and all creation.

   *Me – pride, faithlessness*

   *Not God!*

5. In response to the sin that brought evil into our world, what did God do for us? Read and discuss Ephesians 2:4–10.

   *Kindness towards us "dead in sins" v.17 came + preached peace to you who were far off.*

■ **LIE #2: God doesn't love me.**

■ **TRUTH:** God's love for us is infinite and unconditional. We don't have to perform to earn God's love or favor. He always has our best interests at heart.

■ **LIE #3: God is just like my father.**

■ **TRUTH:** God is exactly what He has revealed Himself to be in His Word. God is infinitely more wise, loving, generous, and kind than any earthly father could ever be.

> NOTE FROM *Nancy*
>
> "The Truth is, God is good. Whether or not His choices seem good to us, He is good. Whether or not we feel it, He is good. Whether or not it seems true in my life or yours, He is still good." (p. 50)

6. Why do people often feel that they need to earn God's love? What part do earthly fathers sometimes play in this understanding?

*Pride; control*

7. Read Romans 8:35–39. How does Paul describe the love of God? What does it mean to you to be loved in this way?

*unloseable = freedom, true freedom*

- **LIE #4: God is not really enough.**
- **TRUTH:** God is enough. If we have Him, we have all we need.

8. What are some of the things you sometimes look to in an effort to fill the empty places of your heart?

*Youtube, sit coms*

9. How might we live differently if we really believed that Christ and His Word were sufficient to meet the deepest needs of our hearts?

*anxiety free; fearless; thankful    Fruits of*
*joy ful; more graceful           the Spirit!*

- **LIE #5: God's ways are too restrictive.**
- **TRUTH:** God's ways are best. His restrictions are always for our good. Resisting or rebelling against His ways brings conflict and heartache.

10. What are some instructions in the New Testament that people might consider burdensome, unreasonable, or unfair? Discuss how those instructions are actually for our good and our protection.

*Be holy for I am holy*

- **LIE #6: God should fix my problems.**
- **TRUTH:** In this world we will have problems and pain. Our pain and heartaches are purposeful and will ultimately be for our good and His glory. God has an eternal purpose He is fulfilling in the midst of my suffering. No matter what difficulty we may be facing, God's grace is sufficient for us.

*God shouts to us in pain*
*It is His megaphone to a deaf & dying world* — C.S. Lewis

11. In what ways does God work through our problems to help us mature in Him? Have you ever experienced this kind of growth through pain? What happened?

*Just a little ....*       *greater knowledge*
*Be of good courage for I have*    *of His character*
*overcome the world . Jn 16:33, 1 Jn 4:4*

12. This chapter quotes Bible teacher G. Campbell Morgan as saying, "The supreme need in every hour of difficulty and distress is for a fresh vision of God. Seeing Him, all else takes on proper perspective and proportion." What is one area of your life that would be different if you were to get a "fresh vision of God"?

*teaching , anxiety*

*forgiveness, grace towards family (unity)*

*"Be still and know that I am God."*

NOTE FROM *Nancy*

*"Our wise, loving heavenly Father says, 'I have a good, beautiful purpose in all of this. I want to use your pain and your problems to change you and to reveal My grace and power to the world.'. . . That's the Truth that sets us free." (p. 62)*

11): A. *Submit to His purposes (eternal view) 2 Cor 4:17*
     B. *God is good and I am not  Job 23:10*
     C. *God is all I need Lam 3:21-24  Col 3:1-4*

# CHAPTER THREE

# SEEING MYSELF AS GOD SEES *Me*

## IN A NUTSHELL . . .

The previous chapter discussed lies women believe about God and explained how what we believe about God affects what we believe about everything else. One crucial area affected is what we believe about ourselves. If we don't believe that God is good, loving, compassionate, and forgiving, we won't be able to believe that He has our best interests at heart or that He loves us, understands us, and can forgive even our deepest, darkest sins. Chapter 3 discusses six lies that many women believe about themselves.

The first lie relates to their worth. Many women feel inferior and worthless because they allow others to decide their value instead of accepting the Truth that, if they are in Christ, they are dearly loved children of God.

The second lie is one we hear on many fronts—namely, that "loving ourselves" will solve all our problems. The problem is that we already love ourselves. That comes naturally. What often appears as a lack of self-love is actually a faulty view of God and our value to Him. We need to learn to receive God's love so His love can fill us and overflow through us to others.

The third lie is found in those self-fulfilling words, "I can't help the way I am." This mindset reduces us to helpless victims. While our circumstances do indeed shape us, we are responsible for the choices we make. If we are children of God, the Holy Spirit lives in us and gives us the power to obey God.

The fourth lie is promoted by a culture that is accustomed to clamoring for "rights." But focusing on our perceived rights only sets us up for disappointment and hurt. True freedom comes when we relinquish our rights and expectations to God.

Fifth is the lie about physical beauty. Many women look at magazine covers and long for such clear skin, such smooth thighs, such a flat stomach, such a perfect nose. The billions of dollars women spend every year trying to look young or become beautiful attest to the power of this lie. While there's nothing wrong with being physically attractive, Christian women ought to be more concerned about cultivating true, inner beauty of the spirit—the kind of beauty that increases rather than diminishes with age.

The last lie focuses on our personal longings. Women who fall for this deception feel that God owes them the fulfillment of their deepest longings. While the longings themselves may not be sinful, the danger is that we will demand that God meet our expectations or that we will seek to meet our desires in sinful ways. By focusing on our unfulfilled longings, we can miss the fact that God by His very presence fulfills the deepest needs of our hearts. Even better, He promises that one day we will lack nothing.

## EXPLORING THE TRUTH . . .

# ACCEPTING GOD'S ASSESSMENT *(pp. 65–71)*

### DAY ONE

### REALIZE

1. Describe a time in your life when you felt on top of the world. Next, describe a time when you felt worthless. What common factors do you find in both experiences? (For example, were your feelings dependent on others' responses to you, on how you looked, on how you performed?)

_____

_____

2. Read Psalm 139:1–18. What do you learn from this psalm about God's heart and thoughts toward you?

_____

_____

### REFLECT

3. Is there someone whose affirmation you crave? Someone whose approval matters a lot to you—perhaps more than it should?

_____

_____

4. How has that longing for human acceptance affected your thoughts? Your emotions? Your behavior? Your relationships with others?

_____

_____

5.  Read Romans 5:6–11. What makes it possible for us, as fallen sinners and enemies of God, to be accepted by God?

_____

_____

NOTE FROM *Nancy*

*"When God sent His only Son, Jesus, to this earth to bear your sin and mine on the cross, He put a price tag on us— He declared the value of our souls to be greater than the value of the whole world. (p. 69)*

6.  What effect do you think a renewed vision of your position in Christ might have on your interactions with family and friends?

_____

_____

_____

**RESPOND**

7.  How can you begin to renew your mind, to understand and trust God's love for you and His acceptance of you through Christ?

_____

_____

*Lord, thank You for loving me so much. Thank You for choosing and saving me.*
*Thank You that through Christ I have been made acceptable to You and am Your*
*treasured possession. Help me to think of myself as Your beloved daughter*
*and to rejoice in the privilege of my relationship with You. Amen.*

# ACCEPTING RESPONSIBILITY *(pp. 72–74)*
## DAY TWO

**REALIZE**

1.  List some of the excuses you've heard people use to explain their wrong behavior (e.g., "My parents got divorced," "We never had much money," or "I never felt loved").

_____

_____

_____

2. Obviously, our upbringing and environment have an effect on who we are. However, these factors don't necessarily *determine* who we are. Negative circumstances don't always mean that a child will turn out badly, nor do positive experiences always mean that a child will turn out well. What do you think makes the difference?

_____

_____

3. Some people live as victims all their lives. What effect does it have on them? Who controls their lives?

_____

_____

_____

## REFLECT

4. Read Colossians 3:1–17. On the basis of who Christ is and what He has done for us (Colossians 1–2), the apostle Paul tells us that we are responsible to make godly choices in every area of life, including our attitudes, our behavior, and our relationships. According to these verses, what are we to "put to death"? What are we to "put on"?

_____

_____

_____

5. In Galatians 5:22–23, what does Paul promise that the Holy Spirit will help to do in our lives?

_____

_____

_____

NOTE FROM *Nancy*

*"This lie—'I can't help the way I am'—can reduce us to assuming we are helpless victims of people and circumstances that we can't change and over which we have no control. The suggestion is that someone or something else is responsible for who we are—that we are like marionettes, destined to be controlled by whoever or whatever is pulling our strings." (p. 73)*

## RESPOND

6. In what area(s) of your life have you been blaming your circumstances, your upbringing, or another person for the way you are, rather than assuming personal responsibility? How do you think God wants you to view that struggle? What fruit of the Spirit (from the Galatians passage) do you need to help you deal with the issue?

_____

_____

_____

*Lord, I agree with You that I am not a helpless victim of my circumstances or my past.*
*I understand I may not be able to change the circumstances of my life,*
*but because of what Jesus has done for me and in me I can control my attitude and my responses.*
*By the power of Your Spirit help me choose to obey You, to take responsibility for my actions,*
*and to be changed into the image of Christ. Amen.*

# YIELDING RIGHTS *(pp. 74–77)*
## DAY THREE

### REALIZE

1. Look at the list of things that many women claim as their "rights" on pages 75–76 of *Lies Women Believe*. While you might wish that all of these things were part of your life, what is the problem with insisting on them as rights?

_____

_____

NOTE FROM *Nancy*

*"In the mid-twentieth century, women were told that demanding their rights was the ticket to happiness and freedom. . . . The fact is, successful relationships and healthy cultures are not built on the claiming of rights but on the yielding of rights."*
(pp. 74–75)

2. When people claim their "rights," how do they respond when those supposed rights are violated? Why does claiming rights so often result in anger, bitterness, depression, and broken relationships?

_____

_____

### REFLECT

3. Read Psalm 37:1–11. What are the attitudes and behaviors of a person who is claiming her "rights"? Describe the attitudes and responses of the person who has yielded her rights and expectations to God?

_____

_____

4. In what area(s) of your life have you tended to think that something was your right (e.g., a healthy marriage, good children, a problem-free church, faithful friends) when it might not truly have been a right at all? Have your assumptions changed in this regard? Why?

_____

_____

## RESPOND

5. Make a list of any "rights" you may still be holding on to, along with any expectations you have placed on others. Consciously surrender each of those "rights" and expectations to God.

_____

_____

*Father, I confess my tendency to defend my "rights"*
*and to become angry, resentful, or impatient when those "rights" are violated.*
*By faith, I yield those "rights" and expectations to You.*
*I trust You to meet my needs and to work out Your purposes for my life. Amen.*

# LASTING BEAUTY *(pp. 78–83)*
## DAY FOUR

## REALIZE

1. Some of the most physically beautiful women are also miserable. Why doesn't physical beauty necessarily make a woman happy?

_____

_____

2. Read 1 Samuel 16:7. What does it mean that God looks at people's hearts?

_____

_____

## REFLECT

3. How would you compare the time and effort you invest in your physical appearance with the time and effort you put into developing a beautiful heart and spirit?

_____

_____

4. Read Proverbs 31:30, 1 Timothy 2:9–10, and 1 Peter 3:1–6. Why is it shortsighted to be preoccupied with external, physical beauty?

_____

_____

NOTE FROM *Nancy*

*"The deception that physical beauty is to be esteemed above beauty of heart, spirit, and life leaves both men and women feeling unattractive, ashamed, embarrassed, and hopelessly flawed. . . . God's Word reminds us of the transitory nature of physical beauty and the importance of pursuing lasting, inner beauty."* (pp. 79–80)

5. According to the passages above, what are the qualities that make a woman truly beautiful to God and to others? How do those qualities affect her outer appearance?

_____

_____

6. How would you describe a balanced and godly approach to your physical appearance? Where would you draw the line between taking care of yourself and trying to look your best, and placing too much emphasis on outward appearance?

_____

_____

## RESPOND

7. How can you develop a heart that reflects true beauty?

_____

_____

*Father, I realize that the most important beauty I can have is the kind that comes from within. Please develop in me that true, enduring, inner beauty that is pleasing to You. Amen.*

# SURRENDERING OUR LONGINGS *(pp. 83–87)*
## DAY FIVE

### REALIZE

1. What are some of your heart's desires that have not yet been fulfilled (e.g., to get married, to improve your marriage, to have children, to find a fulfilling job, to regain health, etc.)?

_____

_____

2. Read Deuteronomy 8:3. Why did God allow His people to go hungry (i.e., to have unfulfilled longings) in the desert?

_____

_____

3. What are some other reasons God might not allow all of His children's longings to be fulfilled here and now?

_____

_____

### REFLECT

4. As you think about the legitimate longings you recorded in question 1 above, consider: have you fallen into the trap of demanding that God fulfill your desires or resenting that He has not chosen to do so? Have you made any sinful choices as a result of trying to meet those longings in illegitimate ways?

_____

_____

5. Read Ecclesiastes 3:11. What does it mean that God has placed eternity in our hearts?

_____

_____

NOTE FROM *Nancy*

*"It's important to understand that our inner longings are not necessarily sinful in and of themselves. What is wrong is . . . when we demand that our longings be fulfilled here and now or insist on meeting those longings in illegitimate ways." (p. 85)*

6. Read Philippians 3:20–4:1. What does it mean that your citizenship is in heaven? What implications do this passage and the verse from Ecclesiastes have as you face what may be legitimate longings that God has not chosen to fulfill?

_____

_____

7. According to Psalm 16:11, where is the only place that all our longings can be completely met?

_____

_____

## RESPOND

8. Elisabeth Elliot reminds us that unfulfilled longings provide "material for sacrifice." On a practical level, how could you offer up one or more of your longings as a sacrifice to the Lord?

_____

_____

*Lord, I have many desires deep within. I understand that those longings are not necessarily bad, but help me not to attempt to meet those longings in wrong ways. Help me to be patient, knowing that You know my longings and that You have my best in mind. Thank You that the day is coming when the deepest thirsts and longings of my soul will be fully satisfied in Your presence. Amen.*

## WALKING TOGETHER IN THE TRUTH . . .

1. In your reading and study of chapter 3, what Truth did you find especially encouraging or helpful? (See pages 88–89 in *Lies Women Believe*.) Did you find any of these Truths difficult to accept?

_____

_____

- **LIE #7: I'm not worth anything.**
- **TRUTH:** Our value is not determined by what others think of us or what we think of ourselves. Our value is determined by how God views us. God paid the ultimate price to purchase us for Himself. If we are children of God, we are His cherished possession and treasure.

- **LIE #8: I need to learn to love myself more.**
- **TRUTH:** By faith, we need to receive God's love for us. God wants us to experience His love and to let Him love others through us.

2. What criteria do most people use to evaluate their own worth or the worth of others?

   _____

   _____

3. We hear a lot about the need for positive self-esteem and the need to learn to love ourselves. How can that kind of emphasis be problematic?

   _____

   _____

4. Read together Luke 12:4–7. Why is it safe to fear God?

   _____

   _____

■ **LIE #9: I can't help the way I am.**

■ **TRUTH:** If we are children of God, we can choose to obey Him. We are responsible for our own choices. We can be changed through the power of His Spirit.

5. Read Romans 6:1–14 and 8:1–2. According to these passages, why are we free to live a life of victory over sin and self? What is our source of power for living this new life?

   _____

   _____

   _____

6. As Paul acknowledges in Galatians 5:17, Christians are engaged in a battle between the flesh and the Spirit. What biblical counsel would you give to a believer who is struggling with sin and says, "I just can't change"? (See 2 Corinthians 5:17 and Galatians 5:16.)

   _____

   _____

   _____

> NOTE FROM *Nancy*
>
> *"If we believe we can't help the way we are, we will never change. We'll go on living in spiritual bondage. And if we believe we are doomed to fail, to keep on sinning or to be miserable, we will fail. We will keep on sinning, and we will be unhappy, frustrated women."*
> (p. 73)

■ **LIE #10: I have my rights.**

■ **TRUTH:** Claiming rights will put us in spiritual bondage. Yielding rights will set us free.

7. Give an illustration of a time when you claimed a right and responded sinfully when that right was violated (e.g., when you were stuck in traffic, when a family member wronged you, etc.).

   _____

   _____

8. How does yielding our rights affect our relationship with God? With others?

_____

_____

9. What is a right or an expectation you were challenged to surrender to the Lord during your study this week?

_____

_____

■ **LIE #11: Physical beauty matters more than inner beauty.**

■ **TRUTH:** At best, as long as we are on this earth, physical beauty is temporal and fleeting. The beauty that matters most to God is that of our inner spirit and character.

> NOTE FROM *Nancy*
>
> *"As Christian women, we have a high and holy calling to reflect the beauty, order, excellence, and grace of Christ, to let others see the difference He makes in our lives. . . . In everything, our goal is to reflect the beauty of Christ and to make the gospel attractive to our world." (pp. 81–82)*

10. Whom do you know who models the beauty of Christ in her spirit? Describe what that looks like.

_____

_____

_____

_____

11. What are some practical ways Christian women can cultivate true, spiritual beauty? How can Christian women make the gospel "attractive to the world"?

_____

_____

_____

_____

_____

■ **LIE #12: I should not have to live with unfulfilled longings.**

■ **TRUTH:** We will always have unfulfilled longings this side of heaven. The deepest longings of our hearts cannot be fulfilled by any created person or thing. If we will accept them, unfulfilled longings will increase our longing for God and for heaven.

12. Read Hebrews 11:13–16. Compare life on this earth to what has been promised to believers. How can a focus on eternity help us live with unfulfilled longings here on earth?

_____

_____

# CHAPTER FOUR

# UNDERSTANDING *Sin*

## IN A NUTSHELL . . .

*C*hapter 4 addresses lies women believe about sin. Many people would like to get rid of the notion of sin altogether. They believe that there is no absolute standard of right and wrong, that truth is a personal matter, and that tolerance is the supreme good. Scripture reveals a holy God whose character determines what is right and wrong. Clearly, sin is real and important to Him—so important, in fact, that He sent His Son to die in order to deal with it once and for all.

What lies do women believe about sin? The first is that people can sin and get away with it. On the surface that may seem to be true, because it appears to happen all the time. In fact, people actually seem to be rewarded for their sin: money, fame, power, and promotions. However, the Truth is that sinners will ultimately receive the consequences of their sin. The pleasures that sin brings us will eventually turn sour.

The second and third lies about sin represent two ends of a spectrum. One lie is that our sin is no big deal; the other is that our sin is so great that not even God can forgive it.

All sin is a breach of God's law, no matter how much we try to rationalize it. While different sins may have more or less severe earthly consequences, any sin is still worthy of death because it is an act of rebellion against God. On the other hand, to believe that our sin is too big for God's mercy is to underestimate the power of the cross.

The fourth lie places responsibility for sin on everyone else's shoulders but our own. We try to excuse our sins, blaming them on an unhappy marriage, character traits we inherited from our parents, or perhaps painful childhood experiences. The Truth is that we are responsible for every choice we make—including our choices to sin.

The last lie in this chapter deals with our attitude toward sin. It suggests that we cannot live in consistent victory from sin. Not true! As believers we have been given the Holy Spirit and a brand-new life. Even though we will struggle with our sinful flesh until the day we die, we are no longer in bondage to sin. We can experience victory over sin because of what Christ has done for us.

# THE TRUTH ABOUT SIN *(pp. 91–97)*

## DAY ONE

### REALIZE

1.  In your own words, define sin.

    _____

    _____

2.  Read Genesis 2:15–3:24. What did God provide for Adam and Eve? Why did God impose such severe consequences for eating a piece of fruit?

    _____

    _____

NOTE FROM *Nancy*

*"Unfortunately, we don't always make the connection between our natural, fleshly choices and the unintended consequences in our lives—whether now or down the road." (p. 95)*

3.  According to Romans 5:12 and 18, what was the effect of the first humans' sin on the world?

    _____

    _____

### REFLECT

4.  Even if no one ever finds out about your sin, who does know? (See Proverbs 5:21; 20:27.) The fear of the Lord involves living in the constant, conscious awareness of the presence of a holy, all-knowing God. How could that awareness protect you from sin?

    _____

    _____

5.  You may not consciously believe that you can sin and get away with it. But we all live as if we believed this lie at times. Give an example of a sin you committed without really stopping to consider what it would cost you.

    _____

    _____

## RESPOND

6. Becoming more conscious of the consequences of sin will help protect us from sin. Based on Scripture as well as your own experience, make a list of several of sin's consequences. You may want to carry that list with you this week so that when you are tempted to sin, you can consider the consequences before you make your choice.

---

*Father, I understand that sin is very real—so real, in fact,*
*that You had to pay the price for my sin with the death of Your Son, Jesus.*
*Lord, You know everything about me: my thoughts, motives, and desires.*
*Help me to be mindful of Your presence in every moment of this day.*
*Guard my heart and keep me from sin, for Jesus' sake. Amen.*

# SEEING SIN FOR WHAT IT IS *(pp. 98–100)*
### DAY TWO

## REALIZE

1. Have you ever compared yourself to other people and thought, "At least I'm not that bad"? What sins in your life seem less important when compared to the sins in others' lives? (Be honest!)

2. Read Galatians 5:19–21. List the "works of the flesh" described in this passage. While different sins may have different consequences, are any of these sins "less sinful" than the others in God's eyes?

> NOTE FROM *Nancy*
>
> *"What may look 'clean' when we compare ourselves to other sinners takes on a whole different cast when seen next to the perfect holiness of God."* (p. 99)

3. According to Romans 6:23, all sin has one ultimate consequence. What is that consequence?

_____

_____

## REFLECT

4. Why did God require blood sacrifices in the Old Testament (see Hebrews 9:22)? How did Jesus' death fulfill this requirement?

_____

_____

5. Consider the price Jesus paid to redeem you from sin. What effect should that realization have on how you view the "little" sins in your life?

_____

_____

## RESPOND

6. What sin(s) in your life have you been trivializing or not really taking seriously? Ask God to give you a greater sense of the sinfulness of sin and what your sin cost Him.

_____

_____

*Lord, I confess that sometimes I forget that there are*
*no "little" sins in Your eyes, and that every sin I commit is an act of rebellion against You.*
*Help me not to excuse my sin but to realize its seriousness and to be truly repentant.*
*Help me to see myself and my sin in the light of Your absolute holiness*
*and the cross of Christ. Amen.*

# SIN AND GRACE *(pp. 100–101)*
## DAY THREE

## REALIZE

1. Some people struggle with receiving God's forgiveness because they feel their sins are just too great. What types of sins do people tend to think are too serious for God to be able to forgive?

   _____

   _____

2. When Jesus died on the cross, what did He accomplish? (See Isaiah 53:6 and John 1:29.)

   _____

   _____

## REFLECT

3. If we think our sins are too big for God to forgive, what are we implying about Jesus' death on the cross?

   _____

   _____

4. According to Proverbs 28:13 and 1 John 1:9, how do we appropriate God's forgiveness? What is the result when we do?

   _____

   _____

5. What types of things do people do in an attempt to "atone" for their sins? What are some of the ways you have tried to "earn" God's favor after you have sinned?

   _____

   _____

6. What would you say to someone who thinks her sins are too big for God to forgive?

   _____

   _____

> NOTE FROM *Nancy*
>
> *"[Many women] find it difficult to accept God's mercy and forgiveness. They feel that in order to be restored into favor and fellowship with God, they need to do something more to atone for their sin; to do 'penance,' to somehow be good enough to make up for the wrong they have done." (p. 100)*

## RESPOND

7. What does God's forgiveness of your sins mean to you?

_____

_____

> *Father, thank You that the blood of Christ is sufficient to cover all my sin. Thank You for offering cleansing and forgiveness to every sinner who comes to You in repentance and faith. Thank You that no sin is too big for You to forgive. By faith, I receive Your forgiveness for every sin I have ever committed. Help me to walk as Your cleansed, forgiven child. Amen.*

# TAKING RESPONSIBILITY *(pp. 101–104)*
## DAY FOUR

## REALIZE

1. Read 1 John 1:5–10. What does it mean to "walk in the light" as it relates to our sin?

_____

_____

NOTE FROM *Nancy*

*"When we are angry, anxious, annoyed, impatient, or fearful, our natural inclination is to try to shift at least some of the responsibility onto the people or circumstances that 'made' us that way."*
(p. 103)

2. Read 2 Corinthians 5:21, which describes Jesus' sacrifice for our sin. What does this verse tell us about the great exchange that God made possible at Calvary?

_____

_____

_____

## REFLECT

3. Are there sins in your life that you have been excusing as mere "weaknesses" or "personality traits"? If so, what are they?

_____

_____

4. Have you been playing the blame game? Are there sins you are committing that you have justified as a reaction to your circumstances or the failures of others (e.g., you blame your husband, your kids, your job, your upbringing)? If so, what are they?

_____

_____

5. Read Psalm 51:1–10. How did David find forgiveness and relief from guilt after he had sinned with Bathsheba?

_____

_____

## RESPOND

6. Reread Psalm 51:1–10 aloud, making it your prayer to God. Accept personal responsibility for any specific sins God has brought to your mind as you have answered these questions. Confess them to Him as sin. (To confess simply means to agree with God about your sin, to call it what He calls it—not a mistake, a problem, a struggle, or a justified reaction to someone else's sin—but sin.)

_____

_____

*Lord, I acknowledge that I am fully responsible for my own actions and choices, regardless of my circumstances or what has been done to me. I know that at times I try to cover my sins by blaming other people or circumstances. Forgive me. Thank You for Your grace that is so abundant when I come to You as a guilty sinner. Amen.*

# VICTORY OVER SIN *(pp. 104–109)*
## DAY FIVE

## REALIZE

1. Salvation does not make us sinless. In fact, Romans 7:15–25 shows that even the apostle Paul struggled with sin. In what ways do you resonate with Paul's words in this passage? According to verse 25, what is the key to experiencing victory over "the law of sin"?

_____

_____

2. According to Romans 8:1–14, what is the role of the Holy Spirit in setting us free from slavery to our flesh?

_____

_____

NOTE FROM *Nancy*

*"You and I are powerless to change ourselves, for 'Apart from me,' Jesus said, 'you can do nothing' (John 15:5). So what are we to do? How can we be set free from habitual sin? It's the Truth that sets us free. And the Truth is that through Christ's finished work on the cross, we can live in victory over sin. We are no longer slaves to sin."* (p. 106)

**REFLECT**

3. Are there any sins in your life that you feel you just can't overcome?

_____

_____

_____

4. How does Christ's work on the cross have the power to set us free from bondage to sin? What truths could you share with a friend who is being defeated by habitual sin?

_____

_____

_____

**RESPOND**

5. Read Galatians 2:20. What does it mean to be crucified with Christ? How does that translate into how you will live today?

_____

_____

6. The first step to walking in victory over sin is to acknowledge that you do not have to live under sin's control (assuming you are a child of God). Talk with the Lord about specific areas where you have continued to give in to sin's control. Thank Him that, at the cross, Jesus broke the power of sin to rule your life. Ask Him to show you how to walk in submission to the Spirit and how to experience the victory that is yours through Christ.

_____

_____

*Father, thank You for Jesus, who came to set me free from sin's bondage.*
*I agree with Your Word that I am no longer enslaved to sin. Help me to live in that freedom.*
*Thank You for Your Spirit, who lives within me and gives me the power to say*
*no to my flesh and yes to You. Amen.*

## WALKING TOGETHER IN THE TRUTH . . .

1. In a sense, the problem of sin is the topic of the entire Bible, which tells how sin began and what God chose to do about it because He loves us. Think about God's character—His love, His justice, His power, and so on. Why does God take sin so seriously? Why couldn't He have said, "I forgive you, Adam and Eve. Let's just put this little fruit-eating episode behind us and move on"?

   *Against His nature ; not just ; messes our r/tnslip up*

2. In your reading and study of chapter 4, what truth did you find especially encouraging or helpful? (See pages 110–11 in *Lies Women Believe*.) Did you find any of these truths difficult to understand or accept?

   *I don't have to sin ; God is training me further away from sin.*

- **LIE #13: I can sin and get away with it.**
- **TRUTH:** The choices we make today will have consequences. We will reap what we sow. Sin's pleasures only last for a season. Sin exacts a devastating toll. There are no exceptions. If we play with fire, we will get burned. We will not escape the consequences of our sin.

3. Many people want to deny the reality of sin. However, that reality is inescapable. How do the consequences listed on pages 96–97 of *Lies Women Believe* manifest themselves in our society today? Does anyone really sin and "get away with it"?

   *Joyless*  ·  *2 Pt 3:9*

4. Share about a situation in which you made a sinful choice ("big" or "small") and experienced consequences you had not anticipated.

- **LIE #14: My sin isn't really that bad.**
- **TRUTH:** Every act of sin is an act of rebellion against God. No sin is small.

- **LIE #15: God can't forgive what I have done.**
- **TRUTH:** The blood of Jesus is sufficient to cover any and every sin we have committed. There is no sin too great for God to forgive. God's grace is greater than the greatest sin anyone could ever commit. *1 Jn 1:9*

51

5. These two lies—"My sin isn't really that bad" and "God can't forgive what I've done"—are opposite sides of the same coin. One <u>trivializes</u> sin; the other trivializes the grace of God. Both diminish Jesus' death on the cross, and both are lies that the Enemy uses to keep us in bondage. Share either a sin in your life that you have tended to shrug off as "not that bad" or a sin for which you have struggled to receive God's forgiveness.

*Complaining "Venting"*

---

6. How does the cross show us the Truth about both of these lies?

*It is that bad!*
*God has forgiven me b/c of what Jesus did*

- **LIE #16: It's not my fault!**
- **TRUTH:** God does not hold us accountable for the actions of others. We are responsible for our own choices.

7. Read the quote on pages 103–104 of *Lies Women Believe* that begins, "Sin is the best news there is . . ." What does the writer mean? In what sense is sin "good news"?

*God has provided an answer,*
*There is hope.*

8. Describe a situation in which you have tried to blame someone or something else for your sin rather than taking personal responsibility for your own choices.

---

- **LIE #17: I cannot live in consistent victory over sin.**
- **TRUTH:** If we are a child of God, we don't have to sin. We are not slaves to sin. Through Christ we have been set free from sin. By God's grace and through the finished work of Christ on the cross, we can experience victory over sin.

9. Why do you think God doesn't just zap us into sinless perfection the moment we receive Christ as Savior?

*Rom 8:17 share in His suffering*

*fluffy fabric*

10. According to Hebrews 10:10, holiness is not something we do, it is something we are because of Christ. How should that truth affect how we live and how we deal with our tendency to sin?

Short accounts; more graceful j less anxious

11. As children of God, we are free from sin's bondage, but our flesh still wars against the indwelling Spirit of God. What are some practical ways we can deal with our flesh and bring it under the Spirit's control every day?

Bible; repentance; pray
quick to acknowledge my sin

Heb 12

2/17/2024

Wares - Misc.
$1.49

White #87

12. What is one area of your life where you are not walking victory over sin? (As women in your group share answers to this question, take time to pray briefly for each one. Encourage someone to pray daily over the next week for each woman who shares a battle with a particular sin in her life.)

Short temper w/students

> NOTE FROM *Nancy*
>
> "What about you, my friend? The Enemy wants to keep you enslaved to fear, doubt, and guilt. God wants [yo]u to walk in freedom, [a]ssurance of [m]atter [m]ay be, [yo]u can [r]ight with God is [...]h faith in Christ. And no matter how great a sinner you may have been, His grace is sufficient for you. Through the death of Christ, God has made the only acceptable provision for your sin." (p. 108)

# CHAPTER FIVE

# SETTING *Priorities*

## IN A NUTSHELL . . .

*I*n this chapter we will consider three lies that many women believe about their priorities. Then we'll discover the corresponding truths in God's Word. Throughout this week you will be encouraged to apply God's Truth to your personal priorities.

The first lie has to do with our many activities and involvements. Look around at the women you know—friends, family, coworkers—or take a quick glance at your own schedule. In spite of countless time-saving devices and conveniences, many of us are living breathless, harried, frazzled lives, convinced that there just aren't enough hours in the day.

The second lie concerns the priority we place on our personal relationship with Christ. Perhaps we think we are just too busy to fit a quiet time into our schedule—or quiet has become a long-lost word in the hustle of our lives. Sometimes we just don't know what or how to go about this devotional time, so we skip it. We think we can keep going. We think we can power through on our own.

The third lie addresses the priority we place on our homes. We've heard it said that home is where the heart is. But, sadly, too often our hearts are pulled everywhere but home. Daily life behind our front doors reveals the fruit of lies as little else can. Despite the culture's cry to elevate work outside the home as most important, God's Word calls us to put the gospel on full display in and through our homes.

**EXPLORING THE TRUTH . . .**

# GOD'S PRIORITIES *(pp. 113–19)*

## DAY ONE

### REALIZE

1. Where do you generally fall on each of the following scales in terms of your priorities, your schedule, and your use of time? Indicate where you fall on the scale in each of the following pairs.

| | | | | | | | |
|---|---|---|---|---|---|---|---|
| Peaceful, calm | 1 | 2 | 3 | 4 | 5 | Stressed, frazzled |
| Well ordered | 1 | 2 | 3 | 4 | 5 | Out of control |
| Purposeful use of time | 1 | 2 | 3 | 4 | 5 | Reacting to life |
| Good steward of time | 1 | 2 | 3 | 4 | 5 | Waste a lot of time |
| Balanced priorities | 1 | 2 | 3 | 4 | 5 | Overwhelmed by demands |
| Fulfilling His "to-do" list for me | 1 | 2 | 3 | 4 | 5 | Frustrated by unfinished tasks |
| Relaxed spirit | 1 | 2 | 3 | 4 | 5 | Uptight spirit |
| Putting "first things first" | 1 | 2 | 3 | 4 | 5 | "Majoring on the minors" |
| Led by the Spirit | 1 | 2 | 3 | 4 | 5 | Driven by others or circumstances |

### REFLECT

2. The word *priority* comes from the Latin word *prior*, which means "first." Our priorities are the things that take "first place" in our time and attention. We all live by priorities—but are we living by the *right* priorities? Are we putting first things first? Read Matthew 6:25–34 and Luke 10:38–42. What are some of the things that compete for "first place" in our lives? What should be the top priority for every child of God?

_____

_____

3. Read Proverbs 3:5–6. What are some of the consequences we might experience if we rely on our own understanding rather than looking to God to order our priorities?

_____

_____

NOTE FROM *Nancy*

*"The Truth is that all I have to do is the work God assigns to me. . . . What freedom there is when I accept that there is time for me to do everything that is on God's to-do list for my day." (p. 116)*

4. According to the verses you just read and Proverbs 2:1–6, how can we discern what responsibilities God is assigning us and what is merely on our own to-do list?

_____

_____

### RESPOND

5. Complete this sentence: "Before I take on additional activities, I will first seek God's guidance by . . ."

_____

_____

6. Write out a brief prayer of commitment expressing your desire to know and do the will of God and to live by His priorities.

_____

_____

_____

*Lord, I want to live according to Your priorities for my life.*
*Please lead me and give me wisdom; teach me what things matter most to You.*
*Help me to make the necessary adjustments in my schedule*
*and to use the days You have given me to fulfill Your agenda. Amen.*

## JESUS' EXAMPLE *(pp. 114–19)*
### DAY TWO

### REALIZE

1. Near the end of His earthly ministry, Jesus said to His Father, "I have glorified You on the earth. I have finished the work which You have given Me to do" (John 17:4 NKJV). What does this verse reveal about Jesus' goals and priorities for His life?

_____

_____

2.  According to Acts 20:24, how were the apostle Paul's goals and priorities similar to those of the Lord Jesus?

    _____

    _____

## REFLECT

3.  If your goal in life is to glorify God and to finish the work He has given you to do, how should that affect your daily schedule and the way you use your time?

    _____

    _____

4.  What helpful insight does Ephesians 2:10 give regarding the specific responsibilities and activities of believers? What difference can this perspective make as you seek to live a well-ordered, godly life?

    _____

    _____

## RESPOND

5.  List the activities in which you are involved in a typical day or week.

    _____

    _____

    _____

6.  Which of the activities you listed above would you consider "optional"? Does each of these activities fit in with your (and God's) priorities for this season? Why or why not?

    _____

    _____

7.  Prioritize each of the optional activities by ranking them with numbers. Are you tending to the top priorities? If not, what can you do to simplify your life so you have time for what is most important? Ask God what adjustments you could make in your schedule to help you glorify Him and fulfill His agenda for your life.

    _____

    _____

8.  What do you need to do in order to be able to go to bed each night and say, "By Your grace, today I finished the work You gave me to do"?

    _____

    _____

*Lord, You know my schedule and all the demands that seem to come at me from every direction. Please help me make wise choices regarding my daily activities, so at the end of the day I can say I have finished the work You have given me to do. Amen.*

## TIME IN THE WORD *(pp. 119–22)*
### DAY THREE

**REALIZE**

1. According to the following verses in Psalm 119, what are some of the characteristics and functions of the Word of God?

v. 9 _____

_____

vv. 25, 28 _____

_____

vv. 50, 52 _____

_____

v. 72 _____

_____

vv. 98–100 _____

_____

vv. 104, 130 _____

_____

v. 165 _____

_____

## REFLECT

2. Read Job 23:12 and Matthew 4:4. What do these verses help us understand about the priority of consistent intake of the Word of God into our lives? In what sense is "feeding" on the Word even more important than eating physical food?

_____

_____

3. Describe your current season of life. (For example, you're chasing toddlers all day, you're working at your job, you're running kids to and from activities, you're an empty nester.) Considering your current season, list below several specific areas in your life where you need God's help, guidance, wisdom, or comfort.

_____

_____

_____

4. As you look over your list, what are some ways the Word of God could meet your current needs?

_____

_____

## RESPOND

5. Considering your intake of God's Word over the past six months, what phrase below best describes your spiritual condition?

☐ seriously malnourished—almost no nourishment

☐ poor diet—subsisting on minimum levels

☐ healthy—consistent, balanced diet

6. What practical action can you take to increase your daily intake of the Word and make your time alone with God a greater priority?

_____

_____

*Lord, I realize my need to spend time in Your Word every day.*
*Please give me a greater hunger to read and meditate on Your Word. Speak to me through its pages.*
*Change my life as I encounter You in Your Word. Amen.*

# TIME IN PRAYER *(pp. 119–22)*
## DAY FOUR

### REALIZE

1. Read Matthew 14:23, Mark 1:35, Luke 6:12, and Luke 9:28. Jesus had a habit of going off alone to pray. Why do you think prayer was such a priority for Him?

   _____

   _____

2. Read 1 Samuel 23:2, 4 and Psalm 5:3. How is David's life an example of the importance of prayer?

   _____

   _____

### NOTE FROM *Nancy*

*"Sometimes I get the sense that God may be saying to me, 'You want to handle this day by yourself? Go ahead.' At best, the result is a fruitless day lived by and for myself. At worst, what a mess I end up making of things! . . . When I start the day by humbling myself and acknowledging that I can't make it on my own—that I need Him— I can count on His divine enabling to carry me through the day."*
*(p. 122)*

### REFLECT

3. Do you have a daily habit of spending time alone with God, reading His Word and praying? If not, what usually gets in the way?

   _____

   _____

4. Think about a day when you tried to "run on your own steam." How did things go? In what ways is your life different when you spend time alone with God?

   _____

   _____

### RESPOND

5. How can you follow Jesus' example regarding time alone with God? (This doesn't necessarily mean you have to get up every day while it's still dark.)

   _____

   _____

6. If you're struggling with having a regular quiet time because you're so busy, try scheduling it. Ask the Lord to show you when is the best time for you. Set that time aside on your calendar for a daily appointment with God.

_____

_____

*Father, I want to cultivate a more intimate relationship with You. Please teach me to pray. Give me the desire and the discipline to spend time each day communicating with You. Amen.*

# THE HEART OF YOUR HOME *(pp. 123–28)*
## DAY FIVE

## REALIZE

1. Read and meditate on Proverbs 31:10–31. These verses present a portrait of a woman whose life is ordered around God-honoring priorities. What can you learn from her about the priorities of a woman who "fears the Lord"?

_____

_____

## REFLECT

2. What are some of the consequences our culture has reaped as a result of women's hearts being lured away from their homes?

_____

_____

_____

> NOTE FROM *Nancy*
>
> *"Daily life behind the four walls of our homes reveals the fruit of lies as nothing else will."* (p. 125)

3. Why is the family so important in God's economy? Why are the roles of "wife" and "mother" so vital in building strong homes?

_____

_____

4. What are some practical ways all women—married or single—can demonstrate the priority they place on nurturing a home that displays the gospel?

_____

_____

## RESPOND

5. Turn to pages 125–26 in *Lies Women Believe* and revisit the list of what "working at home" does not mean in Titus 2. What misapplications of this biblical Truth have you heard or believed?

_____

_____

6. As a part of the body of Christ, how can you encourage other women in their callings as wives, mothers, and keepers of their homes? What are some practical ways you can invest your time and energies in the family of God?

_____

_____

*Thank You, Lord, for the distinctive calling You've given women in relation to their homes.*
*I want to fulfill the role for which You created me.*
*If there are changes I need to make in my priorities, please show me what I need to do*
*and give me the courage to do it. Help me to make my home a haven—*
*a place where You are loved and made known. Amen.*

## WALKING TOGETHER IN THE TRUTH . . .

1. In your reading and study of chapter 5, what truth did you find especially encouraging or helpful? (See page 129 in *Lies Women Believe*.) Did you find any of these truths difficult to accept?

_____

_____

- ■ **LIE #18: I don't have time to do everything I'm supposed to do.**
- ■ **TRUTH:** There is time in every day to do everything that God wants us to do.

2. How can knowing and believing this truth liberate us from false expectations?

_____

_____

3. What are some of the reasons we take on more responsibilities than God intends for us to have?

_____

_____

_____

_____

> NOTE FROM *Nancy*
>
> *"Frustration is the by-product of attempting to fulfill responsibilities God does not intend for us to carry." (p. 118)*

4. Why is it important to consider the particular season of life we are in as we evaluate our priorities? What are the results of trying to do things that are not God's priority for that season?

_____

_____

5. As opportunities arise to add activities to your schedule, how can you decide what is God's priority for you?

_____

_____

6. What role can other believers (husband, parents, godly friends, older women) play in helping us maintain God's priorities for our lives and daily schedules? How can we take advantage of this resource?

_____

_____

- **LIE #19: I can thrive without consistent time in the Word and prayer.**
- **TRUTH:** It is impossible for us to be the women God wants us to be apart from spending consistent time cultivating a relationship with Him in the Word and prayer.

7. Why do you think we often find it so difficult to make Bible reading and prayer a priority in our lives?

_____

_____

_____

> NOTE FROM *Nancy*
>
> *"When our lives are not anchored to Christ and His Word, we become more vulnerable to deception in every area of our lives." (p. 120)*

8. Share your answer to question 5 on page 60 of this study guide. Share any specific commitment the Lord led you to make this week regarding your personal devotional life. (This is a good opportunity to encourage and pray for each other through the weeks ahead.)

- ■ **LIE #20: My work at home is not as significant as the work or other activities I do outside the home.**
- ■ **TRUTH:** Keeping our homes is an important way we glorify God and advance the work of His kingdom. The work we do in our homes is strategic for the gospel.

NOTE FROM *Nancy*

*"What happens inside our front doors, not just outside of them, is an indicator of our spiritual health. Our marriages, our children, and our interactions with guests and neighbors are all to tell the gospel story."*
*(p. 127)*

9. Read 1 Timothy 5:9–10 and Titus 2:4–5. What do these passages tell us about God's priorities for Christian women?

_____

_____

_____

_____

10. Share with each other anything God has been putting on your heart about the need to focus more on ministering to the needs of your family or about using your home for ministry.

_____

_____

_____

_____

# CHAPTER SIX

# UNDERSTANDING GOD'S DESIGN FOR *Sexuality*

## IN A NUTSHELL . . .

*T*his chapter writes you a permission slip to study, discuss, and (if you are married) enjoy God's beautiful gift of sex. Written primarily by author Dannah Gresh, chapter 6 of *Lies Women Believe* identifies five common lies about sexuality that often trip women up.

The first lie zeros in on the shame many women feel as a result of sexual sin. Whether wrestling with sexual addiction (e.g., the use of porn), same-sex attraction, sexual repression (e.g., the inability to enjoy healthy marital sex), or the aftermath of sexual abuse, many women believe the lie that they can't tell anyone about their sexual struggles. The Enemy uses shame to drive them into isolation. But Christ gives the power to bring our sin and shame into the light, to share our burden with others, and to receive healing.

The second lie in this chapter involves the tendency to separate our sexuality from our spirituality and to reduce our understanding of Christian sexuality to a list of rules without grasping the bigger picture of God's design for sex. God's Word gives us that picture and helps us understand *why* He puts protective boundaries around sex.

The third lie cuts to the heart of why sexual sin can be so hard to overcome and why breaking free from its consequences can be so difficult. Lies about sexuality strike at the core of our design as image bearers of God, resulting in the temptation to see our sexuality as something we *are* rather than something we do. God's Word gives us an accurate understanding of our identity, and teaches us that honoring Christ through our sexuality is an important factor in fulfilling our role as His image bearers.

The fourth lie addressed in this chapter deceives women into thinking that biblical standards for sex are out of date. The distorted sexuality of our day is not new. Believers in both the Old and New Testaments encountered similar cultural norms. Yet God called them to a higher standard, and He calls us to this standard of holiness as well. The sexual ethics of Christian women should in no way resemble those of this world. Through His Word, God calls His people to two timeless sexual ethics for our good.

The fifth lie points back to two lies we considered in chapter three: "I have my rights" and "I should not have to live with unfulfilled longings." In the context of sexuality, this lie deceives us into believing that we are entitled to an outlet for our sexual desires and that we cannot live without sex. What we cannot live without is intimacy. We find freedom when we recognize that Jesus is the only One who can ever truly fulfill our deepest longings for true love.

---

## EXPLORING THE TRUTH...

## DEFINED BY THE SAVIOR *(pp. 131–38)*

### DAY ONE

### REALIZE

1. Revisit the list on page 133 in *Lies Women Believe*. Circle any statements you've personally believed. Fill in any other version of this lie that you've believed by completing the prompt below.

   "I can't tell anyone that _____ "

NOTE FROM *Dannah*

*"Satan seeks to shroud our sexual sins, challenges, shortcomings, and fears in shame. But as we see in the very first marriage, there is no shame in healthy, God-honoring sex and sexuality." (p. 133)*

2. Look up Isaiah 64:6. How does this passage describe us in comparison to a holy God? This describes how we may see ourselves when we have sinned sexually: unclean, dirty, and polluted. Yet God's Word offers us an exchange. Flip back a few chapters and read Isaiah 61:10. What does God offer to clothe us in? What do you think these two verses together tell us about what we can do with our "dirty little secrets"?

   _____

   _____

   _____

   _____

3. Read James 5:16. What two action steps does James encourage believers to take? What are the promised results?

_____

_____

## REFLECT

4. Why do you think sexual temptation and sin are so difficult to confess?

_____

_____

5. Read Ephesians 5:11–14. What does the writer of Ephesians encourage us to do with the "fruitless works of darkness?" What promise does this passage make in response to our obedience to drag our sin into the light?

_____

_____

6. Read 1 John 1:7. Compare and contrast what this verse and the Ephesians 5 verses above teach about life in the darkness vs. life in the light.

Life in the darkness means . . .          Life in the light means . . .

| Life in the darkness means . . . | Life in the light means . . . |
| --- | --- |
| | |
| | |
| | |
| | |

## RESPOND

7. Read 1 John chapter 1 aloud as a declaration of your desire to live in the light, keeping nothing hidden in the area of sexual sin.

*Lord, I want to walk in the light because You are in the light.*
*I want to have fellowship with You and with others that is not broken or hindered*
*by sin and secrets. Thank you that Your blood cleanses me from all sin. Amen.*

# EMBRACING GOD'S DESIGN *(pp. 138–42)*
## DAY TWO

### REALIZE

1. Some people think the Bible is relatively silent on the issue of sexuality, leaving us to figure out God's design for ourselves. This is a common misconception, and it couldn't be further from the truth! Look up the following verses. Next to each reference, write down what the Bible teaches about sex.

   Proverbs 5:18–19

   _____

   Ephesians 5:3

   _____

   1 Thessalonians 4:3–5

   _____

   Hebrews 13:4

   _____

NOTE FROM *Dannah*

*"From Genesis to Revelation, the Bible frequently uses language related to marriage and sexual intimacy to inspire our understanding of God's design for sex, and to instruct us as we define Christian sexual behavior." (p. 138)*

2. Write out 1 Corinthians 6:18 in the space below. Circle the one-word action this verse encourages us to take when it comes to sexual sin. Then underline the reason the impact of sexual sin is so devastating.

   _____

   _____

   _____

3. Read Acts 3:18–20. What empowers us to turn from sin? What is the promised result of repentance?

   _____

   _____

   _____

## REFLECT

4. Revisit Genesis 1:26–27. Why did God create biological sex (maleness and femaleness)? When our sexuality steps outside of God's design, what picture is distorted?

_____

_____

5. In what ways have you seen sexual sin in your own life or in the lives of others lead to confusion about the character and will of God?

_____

_____

## RESPOND

6. Read Hebrews 13:4 again. List some steps you can take to honor God's design for your marriage or for the marriages of others.

_____

_____

Now list steps you can take to hold marriage and sexuality in honor in the church.

_____

_____

_____

*Lord, I know that You created sexuality as a masterpiece, designed to reveal something about You.*
*Help me to honor the standards for sexuality outlined in Your Word*
*and to use my sexuality to paint a beautiful picture of who You are. Amen.*

# OUR TRUE IDENTITY *(pp. 143–46)*
## DAY THREE

### REALIZE

1. Sexual sin can result from or lead to a crisis in identity when we confuse our actions (something we *do*) with our design (who we *are*). God's Word is filled with descriptions of our identity that are not based on our actions. Look up the following verses. Next to each reference, complete the "I am" statement that describes who you are according to God's Word.

  • Matthew 5:13–14  I am _____

  _____

  • John 15:15–16  I am _____

  _____

  • Romans 8:14–17  I am _____

  _____

  • Ephesians 2:10  I am _____

  _____

  • 1 Thessalonians 5:5  I am _____

  • 1 Peter 2:9  I am _____

2. Read Colossians 3:3. What happens to our identity when we surrender our lives to Christ?

  _____

  _____

### NOTE FROM *Dannah*

*"The most important thing about your sexuality is not how you feel, but what God says is true." (p. 144)*

### REFLECT

3. In *Lies Women Believe* Dannah describes feeling emotionally paralyzed by her sexual sin. Write about a time when you felt emotionally paralyzed by sin (sexual or otherwise). What truths from God's Word helped you get unstuck?

  _____

  _____

4.  Are there areas of sin in your own life that feel so dominant or permanent that you would say, "This is just who I am"? (Examples could include sexual sin, anger, jealousy, greed, etc.) List anything that comes to mind next to the "I am" statements above. Spend some time comparing the two lists. Ask the Lord to help you see that your true identity is in who He made you to be, not what you do.

5.  Write out Psalm 51:5 in the space below. What does this verse reveal about our identity?

    _____

    _____

## RESPOND

6.  Read Romans 1:1–6. To whom are we called to belong (v. 6)? What do these verses suggest about why we can obey God's commands?

    _____

    _____

*Apart from You, Lord, I will find my identity in all the wrong places.*
*Help me to trust Your Word over my own feelings and agendas. Teach me to live*
*every day in the reality that I have died and my life is hidden with You. Amen.*

# EMBRACING SEXUAL INTEGRITY *(pp. 146–50)*
## DAY FOUR

## REALIZE

1.  What are some of the messages the culture sends about sexuality? (Think about some of the TV shows, movies, songs, and podcasts that are popular right now.)

    _____

    _____

2.  In your own words, summarize the two core commitments that the Scripture calls us to embrace in relation to our sexual practice. (See pages 148–49 in *Lies Women Believe*.)

    #1 _____

    #2 _____

3. What are some differences between the culture's portrayal of a satisfying sex life and the picture we find in God's Word?

_____

_____

_____

NOTE FROM *Dannah*

*"The Designer of sex gets to define our sexual ethic. Put another way: if God truly is the Lord of our lives, He gets to be the Lord of our sexuality." (p. 146)*

**REFLECT**

4. Consider again the statement from the text box on this page: "If God is truly the Lord of our lives, He gets to be the Lord of our sexuality." Write about a time when you made a decision to surrender your will to God's will and to let Him hold the reins of your life.

_____

_____

_____

As you consider God's design for sexuality, is this an area of your life that you've surrendered to His lordship or attempted to retain control of?

_____

_____

5. Revisit the list of nine sexual acts forbidden in Scripture found on pages 148–49 in *Lies Women Believe*. Why do you think God forbids these acts? How does avoiding these activities contribute to human flourishing?

_____

_____

6. If we focus on everything God's Word forbids concerning sexuality, we might get the impression that God is opposed to sex. But nothing could be further from the Truth! As the Designer of sex, God values His design so much that He wants us to enjoy it only as He intended. Read 1 Corinthians 7:3–5. Why do you think God encourages regular sex between married couples?

_____

_____

**RESPOND**

7. Read James 1:5. What promise is extended to believers in this verse? Take some time to ask the Lord to show you His plan for your sexuality and to help you identify any areas of your thinking or behavior that don't align with the sexual ethic outlined in His Word.

_____

_____

*Lord, thank You that You do not change. Your design for sexuality is not impacted by the culture. Give me wisdom to understand Your design. I want You to be the Lord of all of my life, including my sexuality. Help me to make sexual choices that are an expression of who I am as Your image bearer. Amen.*

# TRULY SATISFIED *(pp. 150–55)*
## DAY FIVE

### REALIZE

1. Where have you heard the message that we have a right to have our desires satisfied? (Consider such things as conversations, media, and product marketing.)

2. In *Lies Women Believe* Dannah says sex was designed to be experienced "in a covenant commitment to know and be known." With this in mind, describe why the messages the world promotes are false or inadequate.

3. Read the account of the woman at the well found in John 4:4–30. What words would you use to describe Jesus' connection with the woman?

### REFLECT

4. We are created with a desire to be known. Look up the following passages. Next to each reference, write what God's Word teaches about this desire.

   Psalm 31:7

> NOTE FROM *Dannah*
>
> *"Sexual activity apart from the way God designed it to be experienced—in a covenant commitment to know and be known—is an empty substitute for true intimacy and will never satisfy." (p. 151)*

1 Corinthians 8:3

_____

Luke 12:7

_____

Galatians 4:9

_____

5.  The woman at the well surely knew plenty about sex. What she seemed to have little experience with was knowing and being known—true connection. Once she encountered Jesus, the grip of sex without intimacy was loosened and she declared that she had encountered the Messiah (v. 29). In what ways do you sometimes struggle with trusting God to meet your need for intimacy? How have you sought to meet your need for connection apart from Him?

    _____

    _____

6.  God doesn't just know us; He invites us to know Him. What does each of the following verses reveal about God's desire to be known?

    Psalm 9:16

    _____

    Psalm 16:11

    _____

    Psalm 25:14

    _____

    Psalm 48:3

    _____

## RESPOND

7.  Psalm 139 describes God's intimate knowledge of His creation. Read through the psalm as a prayer, thanking God that He has already satisfied your deep craving to be known.

> *Lord, thank You that You knit me together in my mother's womb.*
> *Thank You that You know the very number of hairs on my head*
> *and the words in my heart before I ever speak them.*
> *My desire to be known is created by You, and You want to satisfy it.*
> *Help me to pursue true intimacy with You and others. Amen.*

## WALKING TOGETHER IN THE TRUTH . . .

1. What specific messages does our culture send about sexuality? What lies about sexuality have you believed?

   _____

   _____

   _____

> NOTE FROM *Dannah*
>
> *"Sin doesn't just happen. We empower it with our own actions. And often those actions are fueled by a belief that's simply not true." (p. 153)*

2. In your reading and study of chapter 4, what truth about God did you find particularly encouraging or helpful? (See pages 156–58 in *Lies Women Believe*.)

   _____

   _____

- ■ **LIE #21: I can't tell anyone.**
- ■ **TRUTH:** Healthy sex and sexuality is free of shame. Guilt is God's tool to bring us back to Him and is free of undue condemnation. Shame is Satan's tool designed to drive us away from God. God designed the Church to help bring healing to those struggling with sin and shame. Our sexual past and current temptations do not define us. The cross does.

3. Revisit Genesis 1:27 together as a group. Bible scholars refer to this passage as the "Imago Dei," pointing to the Truth that mankind was created to reveal the image of God. With this important truth in mind, why do you think the Enemy works to distort holy sexuality in every generation?

   _____

   _____

4. Read Romans 12:21. How does this passage encourage us to fight evil in our world? How can we apply this to combating unholy messages about sexuality?

   _____

   _____

- ■ **LIE #22: My sexuality is separate from my spirituality.**
- ■ **TRUTH:** God created the biological sexes of male and female to reflect something about His image. When one man and one woman join together in marriage and sexual intimacy, they reflect the oneness of God the Father, God the Son, and God the Holy Spirit. Marriage and sex are a picture of the gospel.

■ **LIE #23: This is who I am.**

■ **TRUTH:** Feelings are not facts. Our feelings can be deceptive and wicked. The most important thing about our sexuality is not how we feel, but what God says is true. Our identity is as image bearers of God. Claiming that our identity is in our sexuality denies our purpose to glorify God.

> NOTE FROM *Dannah*
>
> *"If marriage is a picture of our relationship with Christ, we must know the love of Christ in order to paint it. You can't paint a picture of something you've never seen, right?" (p. 154)*

5. In what ways do you see our culture promoting the idea that sexuality and identity are interchangeable?

   _____

   _____

6. Read Colossians 2:6–10. What words does this passage use to describe our walk with Christ? How can we encourage each other to avoid being taken "captive by philosophy and empty deceit" (v. 8)?

   _____

   _____

■ **LIE #24: God's standards for sex are out of date.**

■ **TRUTH:** God's standards were never "in style." Sexual integrity is when our sexual choices are a consistent expression of our relational and spiritual commitments. God does not want us to engage in any form of sex outside of marriage. If we are married, God wants us to engage in regular and mutually pleasing sex with our husband—except when we agree together to abstain for a time of focused prayer.

7. Together read the following passages and discuss what they teach us about the character and standards of God.

   Malachi 3:6

   _____

   Numbers 23:19

   _____

   Psalm 102:25–27

   _____

   How should this information impact our sexual ethics as individuals and as the people of God?

   _____

   _____

- **LIE #25: I have to have an outlet for my sexual desire.**
- **TRUTH:** Our longing for intimacy is legitimate. The physical act of sex is merely an expression of the deeper work of intimacy we long to experience. Our longing for sexual expression can be a snare. Pursuing it apart from God's plan and order will lead to enslavement, not fulfillment. We can live without a sexual outlet, but we cannot live without the unfailing love of God.

8. How have you experienced in your life a craving to be known? Where are some places you've turned other than God in an attempt to meet this need?

   _____

   _____

9. In addition to intimacy, what are some other needs in your life right now (financial, relational, etc.)? Set aside some time to pray for each other about these needs, asking the Lord to give you strength to trust His provision rather than looking to natural or human sources for satisfaction.

   _____

   _____

   _____

> NOTE FROM *Dannah*
>
> "Physical sexual activity in and of itself cannot fulfill your longings for intimacy. Jesus desires to fulfill that need first and foremost with Himself, and then through the gift of appropriate, pure human friendships." (p. 154)

# CHAPTER SEVEN

# HONORING GOD IN MY *Marriage*

## IN A NUTSHELL . . .

This chapter and the next deal with the practical areas of marriage and family. If you are unmarried or do not have children, you may be tempted to skip over these chapters. However, it's important for every believer, in any season of life, to understand the Truth about these topics.

Nowhere is it more challenging to walk in the Truth than inside the four walls of our own homes. And nowhere have most of us experienced greater consequences of deception—hurt, failure, and confusion—than in the area of family relationships. Some of the topics addressed in these chapters are hot-button issues where the teaching of God's Word flies in the face of common assumptions in our culture. The intent of this study is to challenge us to evaluate every area of our lives in light of the Scripture.

If you find yourself struggling with some of the concepts in these chapters, ask the Lord to help you honestly consider whether your beliefs and opinions are based on His Word or on your feelings or the input of others. What's most important is not that you agree with everything in this book, but that you study God's Word and submit yourself to its authority.

Both married and unmarried women struggle with the first lie in this chapter, which equates marriage with happiness. Single women sometimes think that they must get married in order to be happy, while married women may think that their husband's purpose in life is to make them happy. Both lies lead us to look to other people to get our needs met rather than looking to God. People are imperfect and will disappoint us. Only God will never disappoint.

The second lie begins to emerge after a woman marries and realizes that her knight's shining armor has a few chinks and rusty spots. She then sets about to change him, fix him, and make him what she considers a better person. A godly life and prayer are powerful tools a concerned, loving wife can use to help her husband become the man God wants him to be. Even if her husband never changes, she will be sustained by the peace and grace of God. We need God's help to see it's not our job to "fix" our spouse—or our children, friends, or co-workers.

The third lie suggests that a woman has a right to expect her husband to serve her. Of course, a loving husband will want to serve his wife. But if she focuses on how he should help her rather than on how she can bless and serve him, she will experience disappointment and frustration.

The fourth lie introduces the "s" word—submission. Our society has pummeled this word to death, and even many within the church have attempted to sidestep it. However, a wife's submission to her husband is simply the framework designed by our Creator to tell the gospel and to help marriages operate in a healthy manner. It also demonstrates trust in God's ultimate authority over her husband.

The fifth lie is especially pervasive in an era characterized by passive men and aggressive women. Frustrated by husbands who won't lead, many women assume that role by default. In so doing, they may actually exacerbate the problem they're trying to solve.

The sixth and final lie in this chapter has become increasingly common as people come to believe there is no hope for their marriage. The Scripture points us to the Truth about God's purposes and design for marriage, which can enable couples to patiently work through difficulties rather than running from them or throwing in the towel.

**EXPLORING THE TRUTH . . .**

## EXPECTATIONS OF MARRIAGE *(pp. 159–64)*
### DAY ONE

### REALIZE

1. In what ways does our culture promote unrealistic expectations of marriage?

_____

_____

NOTE FROM *Nancy*

*"Women who get married for the sole purpose of finding happiness are setting themselves up for almost certain disap-pointment; they seldom find what they are looking for." (p. 161)*

2. Name an expectation you had prior to marriage that you found to be unrealistic after getting married?

_____

_____

_____

## REFLECT

3. Read Psalms 62:5, 118:8–9, and Jeremiah 17:5–8. Why is it fool-ish to look to people to satisfy us and meet our needs? Where should we focus our expectations?

_____

_____

4. Reflect on your marriage or, if you aren't married, on your desire for a husband. Write down any ways you might be expecting a man to meet needs in your life that only God can meet. If you can't think of any in your life right now, write down how you have seen this dynamic in the lives of others. Pray that God would open your eyes to any such expectations in your heart.

_____

_____

## RESPOND

5. Can you think of any ways you might have made your husband a prisoner of your expectations by putting pressure on him to satisfy you and make you happy? Ask God to help you release your husband in these areas and choose to place your hope wholly in Him.

_____

_____

6. What is the ultimate source of true happiness? What biblical counsel would you give to a woman who says her husband is not making her happy? To a single woman who is finding it difficult to be content without a husband?

_____

_____

*Lord, I thank You for my current situation in life. I pray that You will help me not to look to other people to meet my needs, but to depend only on You. I realize that no human being can control my happiness, but that I can choose to live in joy because of my relationship with You. Amen.*

# LETTING GO *(pp. 164–68)*
## DAY TWO

### REALIZE

1. While our intentions in wanting to change our husbands may be good in our own eyes, what does the Bible say about women who constantly harp on their husbands? (Read Proverbs 17:1; 19:13; 21:9.)

_____

_____

_____

> NOTE FROM *Nancy*
>
> *"When we're obsessed with trying to change our husband or correct what we perceive to be his faults and flaws, we're likely to end up frustrated and resentful. . . . We may also limit God from doing what He wants to do in our spouse. I sometimes wonder how God might move in our mates' lives if we were willing to let Him take over the process." (p. 165)*

### REFLECT

2. Do you feel frustrated by things in your husband's life that you wish would change? If so, how have you been handling those feelings (e.g., ignoring them, ignoring him, nagging, telling your friends, worrying, etc.)?

_____

_____

_____

3. What perspective and hope does Proverbs 21:1 offer about these things that need to be changed in your husband's life?

_____

_____

4. In what ways could living a godly life before your husband be beneficial for both him and you?

_____

_____

5. In what ways can you pray for your husband so that you are truly turning your burden over to the Lord? What Truth(s) from God's Word can help you persevere if you don't see those prayers answered quickly?

_____

_____

## RESPOND

6. Read Matthew 7:1–5. Would you want God and others to deal with your imperfections in the same way you deal with your husband's flaws?

   _____

   _____

7. What "log" may you have missed in your own eye, while you have been focused on trying to get rid of the "speck" in your husband's eye? Ask God to help you see the things in your life that need to be changed.

   _____

   _____

*Lord, I understand that I need to let You work in my life and in the lives of the people I love.*
*Help me not to be nagging, accusatory, or angry. Teach me how to live an upright life*
*and to bring my concerns about others to You in prayer.*
*Help me to wait on You and to trust You to fulfill Your purposes in our lives. Amen.*

# A VIRTUOUS WOMAN *(pp. 168–73)*
## DAY THREE

## REALIZE

1. Read Matthew 20:28; John 13:1–5, 12–17; and Philippians 2:5–7. What does it mean to be a servant? How did Jesus demonstrate the heart of a servant? What do we learn from His example about our calling as His followers?

   _____

   _____

## REFLECT

2. According to Genesis 2:18, God made the woman to be a "helper fit" for her husband. What are some ways a wife might "cooperate and partner with [her husband] in making God known and bringing Him glory"?

   _____

   _____

3. The virtuous woman in Proverbs 31:10–31 is probably a composite of the virtuous qualities in many women. In chapter 5 we looked at her priorities. Now read the passage again and consider what you can learn from her about serving your husband and family. Write down one or two possibilities.

_____

_____

4. How can a woman develop and maintain a servant's heart when she feels that she is being taken advantage of or that no one appreciates what she does? In your opinion, does being a servant always mean doing whatever is asked? Why or why not?

NOTE FROM *Nancy*

*"We are never more like Jesus than when we are serving." (p. 172)*

_____

_____

_____

## RESPOND

5. What are a few practical ways you can demonstrate the servant heart of Jesus toward your husband this week?

_____

_____

6. List some ways that your husband serves you. How can you thank him for those acts of service?

_____

_____

*Lord Jesus, You came to this earth to be a servant. I want to be like You.*
*Yet serving is difficult sometimes; it can be a thankless and lonely job.*
*Help me to serve my husband and family as if I were serving You. Amen.*

# THE POWER OF SUBMISSION *(pp. 173–84)*
## DAY FOUR

### REALIZE

1. Read Ephesians 5:22–33. How should Christian marriages be a picture of the redemptive relationship between Christ and His church?

_____

_____

2. According to verses 22 and 33, what are the two ways wives are called to respond to their husbands?

_____

_____

### REFLECT

3. How does submission to God-ordained authority demonstrate our trust in God?

_____

_____

4. What happens when a woman becomes frustrated with her husband's leadership (or lack of leadership) and takes matters into her own hands? How does that affect her, her husband, and their relationship?

_____

_____

---

**NOTE FROM** *Nancy*

*"Satan has done a masterful job of taking a beautiful, holy, and powerful Truth and making it look ugly, frightening, and undesirable." (p. 174)*

### RESPOND

5. *Married women:* What is an area where you need to pray and wait on the Lord to change your husband's heart rather than jumping in to handle the matter yourself?

_____

_____

6. *Unmarried women*: Even apart from marriage, women can affirm appropriate male leadership by making room for men to take initiative. What is one way you can do this in your relationship with a man such as your father, your employer, or your pastor?

_____

_____

7. *Married women:* How do your responses and your attitude toward your husband measure up to the standard of Ephesians 5?

_____

_____

8. *Unmarried women:* How well are you submitting to whatever human authorities God has placed over you?

_____

_____

*Lord, I confess that I often struggle against submission. Help me to show my submission to You by the way I respond to my husband's leadership. Thank You that even when my husband (or another authority) fails, I can trust You to protect me as I walk in submission to Your Word. Amen.*

# THE COVENANT OF MARRIAGE *(pp. 184–90)*
## DAY FIVE

## REALIZE

1. Read and summarize what the Bible says about marriage in Genesis 2:18–24, Malachi 2:13–16, and Mark 10:2–12. Why is marriage a lifetime, binding relationship? What insight does this give into the Enemy's motivation to destroy God's design for marriage?

_____

_____

_____

2. Revisit the list of questions for a woman who feels hopeless about the restoration of her marriage found on pages 187–88 in *Lies Women Believe*. Respond to any particular questions on this list that God prompts you to consider in light of your own marriage.

_____

_____

## REFLECT

3. Read Psalm 89:33–34 and Isaiah 54:10. What do these verses tell us about the character of God? What are the implications as we seek to reflect His image in our marriages?

_____

_____

NOTE FROM *Nancy*

*"No sooner does a couple say 'I do' than the Serpent rears its ugly head. . . . He knows that every time he succeeds in tearing apart a Christian marriage, this earthly picture of divine redemption is marred."* (p. 185)

4. Review the list of truths about marriage on pages 188–89 of *Lies Women Believe*. In your own words, write out any that apply to a challenge you may be facing in your marriage or that you could share with a friend who is in a difficult marriage.

_____

_____

## RESPOND

5. Take time to pray through these truths. Ask God to help you be faithful to Him and to your mate, no matter how difficult it may feel. In your own words, express below your commitment to reflect the covenant-keeping heart of God in your marriage.

_____

_____

*Note: If you've been divorced, remember that the grace of God can turn "ashes to beauty." He loves you and wants the very best for you. If your husband violated his vow toward you, what steps can you take toward forgiving him and finding healing and wholeness in Christ? To whatever extent you may have been responsible for breaking your marriage vow, what steps can you take to be right with God and with your husband?*

*Thank You, Lord, for being faithful even when we are unfaithful to You. My marriage needs*
*Your presence and power to help us reflect You and bring You glory.*
*Please give me grace to be faithful to You and faithful to my husband.*
*In the difficult times, help me to walk in humility, love, and forgiveness and*
*to trust You to work in our lives and our marriage. Amen.*

# WALKING TOGETHER IN THE TRUTH . . .

1. In your reading and study of chapter 7, what truth did you find especially encouraging or helpful? (See pages 191–93 in *Lies Women Believe*.) Did you find any of these truths difficult to accept? Why?

   _____

   _____

- **LIE #26: I have to have a husband to be happy.**
- **TRUTH:** Being married (or not married) does not guarantee happiness. There is no person who can meet our deepest needs. No one and nothing can make us truly happy apart from God. God has promised to provide everything we need. If He will receive more glory by a woman being married, then He will provide a husband for her. Those who wait on the Lord always get His best. Those who insist on getting what they want often end up with heartache.

2. Why is it dangerous for a woman to think she must have a husband in order to be happy and then to rely on her husband to make her happy? How does having unrealistic expectations for marriage set women up for disappointment?

   _____

   _____

3. How can women who are in difficult marriages find true joy and bring glory to God?

   _____

   _____

- **LIE #27: It's my job to change my mate.**
- **TRUTH:** A godly life and prayer are a wife's two greatest means of influencing her husband.

4. What problems arise when a wife continually focuses on her husband's faults or tries to take God's responsibility for
   changing her husband?

   _____

   _____

5. Read James 5:16 and 1 Peter 3:1. How can we effectively use our tools of godly living and prayer in dealing with our husbands? How will these help them and us?

   _____

   _____

NOTE FROM *Nancy*

*"If you and I focus on what we 'deserve,' on our 'rights,' or on what our spouses 'ought' to do for us, we will become vulnerable to hurt and resentment when our expectations are not met. Blessing and joy are the fruit of seeking to be a giver rather than a taker." (p. 173)*

■ **LIE #28: My husband is supposed to serve me.**

■ **TRUTH:** If we expect to be served, we will often be disappointed. If we seek to serve others without expecting anything in return, we will never be disappointed. A wife has a distinctive calling to be a "helper"—an "indispensable partner"—to her husband. We are never more like Jesus than when we are serving others.

6. Read the "Note from Nancy" quote on this page. Share an illustration of this quote—either an experience out of your own life or one that you have observed in someone else's.

   _____

   _____

■ **LIE #29: If I submit to my husband, I'll be miserable.**

■ **TRUTH:** Through submission, a wife has the privilege of painting a picture of the church's submission to Christ. Through submission, a wife entrusts herself to the One who has ultimate control of her husband and of her situation and is always looking out for her best interests. A wife's respectful, submissive spirit can be a powerful means of influencing a husband who is disobedient to God.

7. What benefits do we experience when we submit to God and to others He has placed in authority?

   _____

   _____

NOTE FROM *Nancy*

*"I have discovered that the fundamental issue in relation to submission really comes down to our willingness to trust God and place ourselves under His authority." (p. 178)*

8. What are some possible consequences of resisting God-ordained authority?

   _____

   _____

9. Share one blessing (or consequence) you have experienced as a result of submitting (or not submitting) to authority?

   _____

   _____

10. In what ways can women emasculate their husbands or other men in authority in their lives by taking the role that the men are supposed to have? What effect could that have on a relationship?

_____

_____

- **LIE #30: If my husband is passive, I've got to take the initiative, or nothing will get done.**
- **TRUTH:** If a woman jumps in to take the reins rather than waiting on God to move her husband, her husband is likely to be less motivated to fulfill his God-given responsibility.

11. When a woman determines to wait on the Lord rather than taking the reins, what blessings could result in her life? In her husband's life? In her marriage?

_____

_____

- **LIE #31: There's no hope for my marriage.**
- **TRUTH:** Marriage is a lifelong covenant that is intended to reflect the covenant-keeping heart of God. There is no marriage God cannot heal. There is no person God cannot change. God uses the rough edges of each partner in a marriage to conform the other to the image of Christ. God's grace is sufficient to enable a woman to be faithful to her husband and to persevere in extending love and forgiveness.

> NOTE FROM *Nancy*
>
> "Christ came to bring hope, to give beauty for ashes (Isa. 61:3), and to reconcile all things to Himself. His Truth has power to redeem, restore, and renew your heart, regardless of what choices your mate may make." (p. 190)

12. Take time to pray together for the marriages represented in your group. (If your group is too large or you are under time constraints, you may want to pray in smaller groups or exchange names to pray for each other during the week ahead.)

- Pray that each marriage would bring glory to God and would become a picture of His redeeming love.

- Pray that each partner represented would accept and live out God's role for him or her in the marriage.

- Pray for spiritual protection from every form of deception and from the schemes of Satan.

- Pray for those marriages that are struggling. Ask God for humility and grace to work through any issues that are undermining or threatening the oneness of the relationship.

# CHAPTER EIGHT

# RAISING *Children*

## IN A NUTSHELL . . .

God created women with the unique ability to bear and nurture children. Chapter 8 deals with several subtle lies and half-truths about children and parenting that are widely accepted in our culture today. It's easy for us as Christian women to adopt the world's way of thinking without stopping to consider how those beliefs line up with God's Word. I've attempted to share in this chapter my understanding of what the Scripture teaches. My primary concern, however, is not that you agree with me on every point, but that you make the effort to study the Word for yourself and make sure your beliefs and practices are rooted in Truth.

The first area of deception is in relation to childbearing. In various ways, the world communicates that children are a burden and that each woman has the right to determine if and when she will have children. God's Word teaches, on the other hand, that children are a blessing, a gift from God, and a vital part of His plan for passing the Truth on to the next generation. As we trust God in other areas of our lives, so we can trust Him regarding the timing and size of our families.

The second lie cuts to the heart of our trust that God can provide for our needs, no matter what size family we have. The message young women are hearing—loud and clear—is that raising kids is prohibitively expensive and a large family is a luxury few can afford. But the Truth we find in Scripture is that if God sees fit to bless a family with children, He will also bless them with all thay need to raise those children for His glory.

The third lie is actually two opposite lies, both of which put parents in bondage. On one end of the spectrum, Satan deceives parents with the idea that they have no influence over how their children turn out—that many children will inevitably rebel and that they must be allowed to find their own way. On the other end, he leads parents to believe that they are totally responsible for how their children turn out, so it is the parents' fault if the children stray. We need parents who love the Truth and who will lead their children to love

Christ, praying that the Spirit of God will capture these young hearts and that they will reflect His glory to the next generation.

The fourth lie identifies the danger of being a religious "helicopter parent." The Bible teaches that it is part of our fallen, human nature to set up idols in our hearts. This can include good things like children and the parenting role. The Bible is clear about the high, holy calling of motherhood, but also makes clear that a mother's love for her children should never outweigh her love for Jesus. A mom's highest priority is loving and following Him—and that means her children do not come first.

The final lie in this chapter calls for a time-out in the "mommy wars" and warns against sinful comparison. Rather than weighing their performance against standards created by the media, mommy bloggers, child experts, and friends, the Bible urges mothers to humbly and honestly hold up their parenting efforts before the Lord for His scrutiny. God's Word also reminds us to flee from envy and pride, extending grace and understanding to other moms.

**EXPLORING THE TRUTH . . .**

## THE BLESSING OF CHILDREN *(pp. 195–203)*
### DAY ONE

*Note: Feel free to skip any questions in this chapter that do not apply to your current season of life.*

**REALIZE**

1. Read the following verses: Psalms 113:9, 127:3–5, and Matthew 19:13–15. What do they tell us about God's view of children?

   _____

   _____

2. How is the world's view of children different than God's view?

   _____

   _____

NOTE FROM *Nancy*

*"The process by which most couples—even believers—determine the size of their family is often driven by the assumption that they simply don't have the financial, emotional, physical, or time resources to add another child (or any children at all) to their lives." (p. 204)*

## REFLECT

3. Why do you think the topic of having children evokes such intense feelings and reactions from many women?

_____

_____

4. What are some of the factors that commonly influence people's decisions about the size and timing of their families? Circle any factors that have influenced your decisions in this area.

_____

_____

_____

5. God's Word has much to say about children and childbearing—for example:

- Children are a blessing and a gift from God (Psalm 127:3–5).

- Children are a primary means of passing the faith from one generation to the next (Psalm 78:1–7).

- God is the One who opens and shuts the womb; childbearing is a primary purpose of marriage (Malachi 2:15).

- The willingness to bear children is a vital evidence of a woman's faith (1 Timothy 2:15; 5:14).

We also know that God is sovereign and that He can be trusted (Jeremiah 29:11). What implications would these truths have for a couple as they make decisions related to childbearing?

_____

_____

## RESPOND

6. Put a check next to each word or phrase that best describes your general perspective and approach to childbearing.

| | |
|---|---|
| ☐ fear | ☐ faith |
| ☐ natural, human reasoning | ☐ biblical thinking |
| ☐ selfish motives | ☐ a commitment to the kingdom of God |
| ☐ personal emotions and desires | ☐ a sincere desire to honor God |

7. Sometimes it's easy to forget that children really are a blessing from the Lord! If you have children of your own, write their names and ages below. Next each name, write a phrase or two explaining how that child has been a blessing to you. If you don't have children of your own, write the names of children who are in your life and the ways they have blessed you.

_____

_____

_____

_____

8. Can you think of any ways you could more fully embrace God's good purposes and plan in relation to children and childbearing, in this season of your life?

_____

_____

_____

_____

*Lord, thank You for the gift of children. Help me to welcome them as You do. Show me how to fulfill my calling as a woman—to be a bearer and nurturer of life, whether that means having physical children of my own or "mothering" spiritual children You entrust to me. Amen.*

# WELCOMING CHILDREN *(pp. 204–208)*
## DAY TWO

### REALIZE

1. Read Genesis 22:1–14. What did the Lord ask Abraham to do to his son, Isaac? Why did Abraham obey?

_____

_____

2. Revisit verse 14. What did Abraham call the site where he found a ram tangled in the thicket?

_____

_____

The Hebrew term used in this passage is *Jehovah Jireh*, meaning "The Lord will provide." That day on the mountain, Abraham learned an important lesson that can be applied by all parents: God is the ultimate provider for parents and children.

3. Look up the following verses. Beneath each reference, write what you learn about God's role as your provider.

   Psalm 145:16

   _____

   Psalm 146:7–9

   _____

   Matthew 6:26

   _____

   Philippians 4:19

   _____

NOTE FROM *Nancy*

*"The Lord Jesus modeled a vastly different value system when He welcomed children into His life, took time for them, and urged His followers to do the same."*
*(p. 206)*

**REFLECT**

4. What are some of the messages our culture sends about children? Make a list below.

   _____

   _____

   _____

5. Read Matthew 19:13–15. How would you describe Jesus' attitude toward children? How is this different from the cultural messages you've seen and heard about children and parenting?

   _____

   _____

6. When the angel told Mary she would conceive and bear a Son, she responded: "I am the Lord's servant. May it be done to me according to your word" (Luke 1:38 csb). Prayerfully consider whether that is the attitude of your heart in any of the following areas that relate to your current season of life:

   • The timing for starting a family

   • The timing for deciding to stop having more children

   • The number of children you are willing to conceive/raise

   • Intentionally investing in the lives of children and families

   • Passing the baton of faith on to the next generation

## RESPOND

7.  We can rest in the Truth that God will care for us and any children He entrusts to us. In the space below, write out a prayer telling God that you trust Him to meet your needs. If there are areas where you're struggling to believe He can provide, confess your doubt. Ask God to help you rest in His care for you and your family.

_____

_____

> *Lord, I know You can provide for the needs of my family.*
> *Help me to trust You and to surrender my will to Yours. Amen.*

# THE IMPACT OF A GODLY PARENT *(pp. 208–16)*
## DAY THREE

## REALIZE

1.  Children are a valuable treasure; they must be carefully protected, cared for, and nurtured. As you would protect a delicate seedling from winter storms and regularly give it water, what are some things you can do to care for the precious "seedlings" (children) in your life?

    • Protect them:

    _____

    _____

    • Give them what they need:

    _____

    _____

2.  Read Psalm 101. In your own words, summarize what this psalm suggests about the environment parents should seek to create and maintain in their home.

    _____

    _____

3.  Read Psalm 92:13–15. What encouragement do these verses give to parents who seek to raise their children in a Christ-centered environment?

    _____

    _____

## REFLECT

4. While God does not intend for us to know evil by experiencing it ourselves, He does want us to understand that evil exists and to learn to discern between right and wrong. How can parents help their children develop this kind of discernment without exposing them to influences from which they should be protected?

_____

_____

5. Read Matthew 5:13–16. What are some practical ways you can give your children a vision for becoming an influence for righteousness in our world?

_____

_____

## RESPOND

6. What character and spiritual qualities do you want your children to have when they leave home? How can you be more intentional about developing those qualities in their lives?

_____

_____

NOTE FROM *Nancy*

*"The persevering prayers of a righteous mom (or grandmom, aunt, or friend) can make a profound difference in a child's life." (p. 215)*

7. Biological children often resemble their parents physically. If your children were to end up resembling your heart and character, what would they look like? What changes do you need to allow the Lord to make in your life so you can say to your children, "Imitate me, just as I also imitate Christ" (1 Corinthians 11:1 NKJV)? (If you're really courageous, ask your older kids to answer these questions about their mother!)

_____

_____

_____

*Lord, it's sobering to realize how much our children pick up from our lives, our values, and our walk with You. Please make me a woman who reflects You to the next generation. May my life create in them a desire to know and follow You. Please work in their lives to draw them to You, that they may reflect Your light to others. Amen.*

# GOD-CENTERED PARENTING *(pp. 216–19)*
## DAY FOUR

### REALIZE

1. In this chapter we learned that an idol "is anything we want more than God, anything we rely on more than God, anything we look to for greater fulfillment than God."[1] With this definition in mind, summarize the warnings found in the following Scriptures.

   Exodus 20:3–6

   _____

   1 Corinthians 10:14

   _____

   1 John 5:21

   _____

2. Considering what gets the most of your time, energy, money, attention, and affection, put a plus sign (+) next to any of the following that need to be a higher priority in your life. Put a minus sign (–) next to any that need to be a lower priority.

   ___ My marriage
   ___ My job
   ___ My children
   ___ Volunteer work
   ___ My home
   ___ Health/physical fitness
   ___ Social media
   ___ Entertainment/recreation
   ___ Friendships
   ___ My relationship with Christ

   > NOTE FROM *Mary*[2]
   >
   > *"Your love for your children should never outweigh your love for Jesus." (p. 217)*

   What adjustments need to be made to your schedule, your spending, or your heart in order for knowing and loving Jesus to be your top priority?

   _____

   _____

---

1. Nancy Pearcey, *Finding Truth: Five Principles for Unmasking Atheism, Secularism, and Other God Substitutes* (Colorado Springs, CO: David C. Cook, 2015), 36.
2. The final two lies in chapter 8 in *Lies Women Believe* were written by my friend Mary Kassian.

**NOTE FROM *Nancy***

*"[The Lord] doesn't want your world to revolve around your children; He wants you to engage your children in a lifestyle that revolves around His kingdom."* (p. 217)

## REFLECT

3. Why do you think some women are prone to idolize their families?

   _____

   _____

4. What other root lies feed into the lie that "my children are my number-one priority"? For guidance, revisit the lies listed in the table of contents for *Lies Women Believe*.

   _____

   _____

## RESPOND

5. Look on pages 218–19 of *Lies Women Believe* and consider the list of ways to send the message that the Lord is the center of a family's life. How could you send this message to your family? Circle any ideas that you plan to implement this week.

   _____

   _____

6. Confess any area of idolatry the Lord may have exposed in your life. Ask the Lord to help you prioritize your love for Him above all things.

   _____

   _____

*Jesus, You are worthy of my time and affections. I want You to be first in my life.*
*Thank you for the many gifts You've given me, including my family.*
*Help me to love others well as an outflow of loving You first. Amen.*

# WAVING THE WHITE FLAG *(pp. 219–24)*
## DAY FIVE

### REALIZE

1. Where have you seen evidence of "mommy wars"? How have you experienced this conflict in your own life?

_____

_____

2. Consider whose approval you tend to seek most often in the following areas. Answers could include your husband, parents, children, friends, social media followers, other women, or the Lord.

The décor and organization of my home _____

My discipline strategies _____

Our family schedule _____

The size of our family _____

Type of schooling chosen for my children or myself _____

Work/child-care arrangements _____

Now read Galatians 1:10. Whose approval are we to seek first and foremost in our lives?

_____

_____

_____

> ### NOTE FROM *Mary*
> *"Be a grace giver. Stop arguing about parenting opinions, and stop criticizing and looking down on those with differing opinions." (p. 224)*

3. Read Romans 12:3. After prioritizing the will of God, who are we to consider next when making choices? What might this mean practically about how you make decisions for your family?

_____

_____

## REFLECT

4. Consider a time when you felt judged by another mom. What happened, and how did it feel? Now consider a time when you felt or acted judgmental toward another mom. Considering the Truths found in this chapter, how do you wish you had responded to those situations differently?

_____

_____

_____

5. Read Proverbs 29:25. How does this verse describe the fear of man? Can you think of a situation in which you were ensnared by the fear of what others would think of you?

_____

_____

6. Fear of man isn't a switch we can simply switch to the "off" position. Instead, we must replace it with a healthy, holy fear of the Lord. Look up the following verses. Next to each prompt, write what you learn about the fear of the Lord.

    Deuteronomy 10:12

    _____

    Psalm 33:8

    _____

    Proverbs 1:7

    _____

    Proverbs 14:26

    _____

    Ecclesiastes 12:13

    _____

## RESPOND

7. Consider a mother in your world who could use some encouragement. Take it a step further and choose a woman whose parenting choices you've sometimes questioned. Write her a note letting her know that her role as a mother is important and tough, and that you appreciate the investment she is making in the lives of her kids.

    _____

    _____

8. Make a list of a few moms you know who are in a difficult season, and commit to pray for them as the Lord prompts over the next week.

_____

_____

*Father, thank You that You designed motherhood as a way to nurture life and*
*pass the baton of faith on to the next generation.*
*Help me to see children as You see them—as a blessing.*
*I trust You to provide for my family in every way.*
*Help me to represent the calling of motherhood well. Amen.*

## WALKING TOGETHER IN THE TRUTH . . .

1. In your reading and study of chapter 8, what truth did you find especially encouraging or helpful? (See pages 225–27 in *Lies Women Believe*.) Did you find any of these truths difficult to accept?

_____

_____

- **LIE #32: I have the right to control my reproductive choices.**
- **TRUTH:** God is the Creator and Giver of life. He is ultimately in charge of a woman's body and her fertility. He is the One who opens and shuts the womb. Life begins at conception. Abortive methods of contraception are the taking of a life.

2. Read Psalm 127:3–5. Why are children called a "reward"? In what ways have you experienced this to be true?

_____

_____

3. In what ways does the world sometimes discourage women from having children? How can Christian couples demonstrate the value God places on children?

_____

_____

NOTE FROM *Nancy*

*"If He sees fit to bless you with children, He will also bless you with all you need to welcome them and raise them for His glory." (p. 208)*

- **LIE #33: We can't afford to have any more children.**
- **TRUTH:** Children are a blessing from God and a fulfillment of the command of God to multiply and fill the earth. One of the purposes of marriage is to produce "godly offspring." The Lord will provide everything a woman needs to raise and provide for any children He gives her.

4. What biblical encouragement would you give to a woman who wants to have more children but whose husband thinks they have enough already?

_____

_____

- **LIE #34: I can't control/can control the way my children turn out.**
- **TRUTH:** God promises a blessing to parents who keep His covenant and who teach their children to do the same. Parents cannot force their children to walk with God, but they can model godliness and cultivate a climate in the home that creates an appetite for God and is conducive to the spiritual nurture and growth of their children. Parents who assume their children know the Lord, regardless of their lifestyle, may give their children a false sense of security and may not be praying appropriately for their children.

NOTE FROM *Nancy*

*"The first lie is that parents have no influence over how their children turn out. . . . The second lie is that parents are totally responsible for how their children turn out—that it is their fault if their children stray."* (p. 209)

5. What kinds of influences in our culture do you think are particularly harmful to young children? How can Christian parents protect their children from unnecessary exposure to those influences?

_____

_____

6. In what ways can Christian parents help to cultivate in their children an appetite for God's Word, His Truth, and His ways?

_____

_____

7. What are some ways parents can keep the lines of communication open during the changes and challenges of the teen years?

_____

_____

8. Why is prayer such a powerful resource for moms (and for all who care about the hearts of children and prodigals)?

_____

_____

■ **LIE #35: My children are my number-one priority.**

■ **TRUTH:** Loving and serving God is our highest priority. It is possible to sin by loving our children more than we love the Lord. Children are taught to put God first by watching their parents put God first. Children need to be trained to be selfless rather than selfish.

■ **LIE #36: I'm not/she's not a good mother.**

■ **TRUTH:** The sin of comparison leads to pride and envy. Ultimately, every mom is accountable to the Lord for her parenting choices. Accepting other believers whose parenting opinions on non-essential matters differ from our own brings glory to God.

9. Read Deuteronomy 6:4–9 and Proverbs 4:11. What does the Scripture say about the importance of parents providing both a good example and solid instruction for their children?

_____

_____

10. What are some ways the people of God (whether or not they have children of their own) can express God's heart for children and cultivate in the next generation a love for Christ and His kingdom?

_____

_____

11. Take time to pray (by name, if possible) for the children represented in your group.

- Ask the Lord for wisdom and grace for each mother to know how to influence and mold her children's lives.

- Pray that the Holy Spirit will graciously intervene in the children's lives, bringing each to true salvation. Pray that each child will be protected from any harmful influences and will develop a love for righteousness and a hatred for evil.

- Pray that God's eternal purposes will be fulfilled in each child's life and that the baton of faith will be passed on intact to the next generation.

> NOTE FROM *Nancy*
>
> *"Even the best parents are utterly dependent on the Holy Spirit to do a work in their children's hearts. That's why a mother's most powerful resource is prayer."*
> *(p. 215)*

# CHAPTER NINE

# HANDLING *Emotions*

## IN A NUTSHELL . . .

*I*n chapter 9 we come to one of the most complex and difficult-to-understand aspects of our walk as women—our emotions. God created emotions. He experiences emotions and understands them. However, His emotions are always perfect, whereas ours have been tainted by sin. Our emotions can send us all kinds of mixed messages, often deceiving us and leading us away from the Truth. Further, Satan lies to us about our emotions to confuse us. The best weapon against this is to pinpoint the lies and learn to counteract them with the Truth.

The first lie tells us that if we feel something, it must be true. If we feel unloved, then we are. If we feel that God has deserted us, then He has. The Truth that counteracts this lie is that we can't depend on our feelings to give us an accurate assessment of reality. Regardless of how or what we may feel, we need to learn to rely on what we know to be true.

The second lie convinces us that we cannot control our feelings, effectively allowing them to run our lives. We sometimes use this belief to justify wrong actions or reactions on our part, rationalizing, "I can't help the way I feel." While it's true that we cannot necessarily control how we feel about something, we can control how much power we allow our feelings to have. We can always choose to obey God, regardless of how or what we are feeling.

The third lie sometimes gets us off the hook when we're responding in ungodly ways. We may use our changing hormones as an excuse for sinful words or actions: "I can't help it . . . It's my hormones." Or "It's that time of the month." Or "It's these awful hot flashes." The Truth is that sinful behavior is never justified, regardless of what may be taking place in our bodies. As our Creator, God understands the hormonal changes associated with the changing cycles and seasons of our lives. His grace is available and sufficient to help us obey and glorify Him as we pass through every season of life.

The fourth lie has to do with how women deal with the problem of depression. This is a real, painful, and complex issue for many women. But even more perilous than the depression are the lies and half-truths the Enemy spreads about depression. Regardless of how we are feeling or what we are going through, our first response should be to turn to the Lord, who provides grace for those who cry out to Him in their distress. His Truth is the first line of defense for all that ails us, including depression. God has not promised to provide ultimate relief for all our problems here and now. But He has promised to be with us and to give us grace to endure. He has also given us other believers to come alongside and minister to us in our need. Our goal, even in the darkest, deepest valleys, should be to bring glory to Him and to allow Him to sanctify us through our pain.

## EXPLORING THE TRUTH . . .

# DISCERNING YOUR EMOTIONS *(pp. 229–32)*
## DAY ONE

### REALIZE

1. Read Deuteronomy 4:24, Psalms 30:5 and 36:5, and Matthew 26:38. According to these verses, what are some of the emotions God experiences? Why is it important to understand that God has feelings and expresses them?

_____

_____

2. If we are made in God's image (Genesis 1:27), what does that tell us about our emotions?

_____

_____

### REFLECT

3. Read Psalm 16:5–11. What words or phrases in this passage speak of positive emotional expressions? What causes such emotions to flow out of the psalmist's heart?

_____

_____

_____

NOTE FROM *Nancy*

*"The Truth is that, due to our fallen condition, our feelings often have very little to do with reality. In many instances, feelings are simply not a reliable gauge of what is actually true. . . . If we want to walk in freedom, we must realize that our emotions are not necessarily trustworthy and be willing to reject any feelings that are not consistent with the Truth." (p. 231)*

4. In what ways are our emotions tainted by the fall? Give some examples of how you have experienced that tainting of emotions in your life.

_____

_____

_____

5. What are some of the factors that can cause our feelings to fluctuate?

_____

_____

_____

6. Why is it dangerous for us to live and act completely on the basis of our feelings?

_____

_____

_____

7. Read Psalm 56:3–4. What is the role of faith in dealing with our emotions?

_____

_____

## RESPOND

8. What is one feeling you have experienced recently that is not consistent with the Truth and needs to be brought into submission to the Truth?

_____

_____

*Lord, I understand that my emotions are part of how You created me,*
*yet many times they are unreliable because they are influenced by changing*
*circumstances or by my human weakness.*
*Help me to reject any feelings that are not based on Truth*
*and to trust Your Word rather than my feelings. Amen.*

# CONTROLLING YOUR EMOTIONS *(pp. 233–36)*
## DAY TWO

### REALIZE

1. Describe a time when your emotions got the better of you—when you felt that they were out of control.

   _____

   _____

2. How much do your emotions affect your actions on any given day?

   _____

   _____

### REFLECT

3. Ephesians 4:26 says, "Be angry and do not sin." The Bible acknowledges the reality of anger, but God expects us to control how we react when we are angry. The emotion of anger itself is not a sin, but it can prompt a sinful response. Which emotions do you have the hardest time controlling? What are some sinful ways you tend to express those emotions?

   _____

   _____

4. Read Isaiah 26:3, Philippians 4:8–9, and Colossians 3:1–2. How can we be free from bondage to feelings that are not based on Truth? Why is it so important to control what we think about?

   _____

   _____

5. What positive steps does the Scripture exhort us to take in dealing with runaway emotions?

   _____

   _____

### RESPOND

6. What can you do today to fix your mind, thoughts, and heart on God and His Truth?

   _____

   _____

*Father, sometimes my emotions seem overwhelming.*
*Thank You that I do not need to be controlled by them.*
*I pray that You will be Lord over every part of my life, including my emotions.*
*Help me to set my thoughts and affections on You each moment of the day. Amen.*

# EXPRESSING YOUR EMOTIONS *(pp. 233–36)*
## DAY THREE

### REALIZE

1. The Psalms often express deeply personal outpourings from the psalmists' hearts. What emotions are expressed in the following verses?

   Psalm 6:1–3                                           Psalm 51:1–2

   _____                              _____

   _____                              _____

   Psalm 9:1–2                                           Psalm 90:7–10

   _____                              _____

   _____                              _____

   Psalm 10:1                                            Psalm 118:24

   _____                              _____

   _____                              _____

### REFLECT

2. In each of the passages above, the psalmist pours out his heart to the Lord. Why is that significant?

   _____

   _____

3. Read all of Psalm 6. How does David bring God into his emotional struggle? How can expressing our feelings to God help us deal with runaway emotions?

   _____

   _____

4. What Truths about God helped David find emotional stability in Psalm 6?

_____

_____

_____

> NOTE FROM *Nancy*
>
> *"The Scripture is filled with promises and commands that provide the means by which our emotions can be steadied in the midst of any storm." (p. 234)*

5. Read 2 Peter 1:4. How can God's promises protect us from expressing our natural emotions in sinful ways?

_____

_____

_____

6. Write down a promise from God's Word that you can turn to and rely on when you are feeling overwhelmed by negative emotions.

_____

_____

## RESPOND

7. Review the list of promises and commands from God's Word on pages 234–35 of *Lies Women Believe*. Which promise or command can you hold on to or obey today to help steady any emotions you may be feeling that are not based on the Truth?

_____

_____

> *Thank You, Father, that I can pour out my heart to You when I am troubled.*
> *Thank You for the many promises and commands in Your Word that can protect me from sin.*
> *Help me to claim Your promises and look to You for grace to obey Your commands,*
> *regardless of what I may be feeling. Amen.*

# FACING LIFE'S CHANGING SEASONS *(pp. 236–40)*
## DAY FOUR

### REALIZE

1. Describe what happens to you during "that time of the month" (if you are in that season of life). What physical and emotional changes do you tend to experience during that time? (If you are pregnant or menopausal, describe what is going on with you.)

_____

_____

2. How do you typically respond to the changes you listed above? Do your actions and reactions generally affect your relationships positively or negatively? Explain.

_____

_____

| NOTE FROM *Nancy* |
| --- |

*"Is it conceivable that this wise, loving Creator would be unaware of our hormone levels at any stage of maturity or would have failed to make provision for every season of life? He does not offer an easy or trouble-free process of growth. But He has promised to meet all our needs and to give us grace to respond to the challenges and difficulties associated with every stage of life."* (p. 239)

3. In what ways do you tend to excuse your behavior—in your own mind, or aloud to others—when you don't feel well physically?

_____

_____

### REFLECT

4. Read Psalm 139:1–18 and Luke 12:7. How well does God know you—your body, mind, and circumstances? How is His intimate knowledge of you comforting?

_____

_____

5. List some divine resources that are available when your body is changing and you feel out of control (e.g., the grace of God).

_____

_____

## RESPOND

6.  What practical steps can you take to ensure that, even if you are experiencing physical changes and your emotions are swinging wildly, you don't act in a way that is displeasing to God or unloving toward others?

_____

_____

_____

*Lord, I sometimes find it difficult to respond to You and to others in a godly way,*
*when certain changes are taking place in my body. I know that You created me, that You control*
*the changing cycles and seasons of my life, and that You have the resources to help me through.*
*Help me to honor You in each of those seasons. Amen.*

# DEALING WITH DEPRESSION *(pp. 241–51)*
## DAY FIVE

## REALIZE

1.  Read Psalm 42. Describe some of the circumstances David was facing and how he was feeling when he wrote this psalm.

_____

_____

2.  Which verses in this passage show that David . . .

    *   was honest with God about how he was feeling?

    _____

    *   made himself face the root issues of his depression?

    _____

    *   turned to God in his depression?

    _____

    *   counseled his heart according to the Truth of God's character?

    _____

• exercised faith in God's ultimate victory over his feelings and circumstances?

_____

## REFLECT

3. The Scriptures indicate that spiritual and heart issues can actually produce physical and emotional symptoms of depression. Select two or three of those issues from the list below and explain how they could contribute to symptoms of depression.

Ingratitude

_____

Unresolved conflict

_____

Guilt

_____

Bitterness

_____

Unforgiveness

_____

Unbelief

_____

Claiming of rights

_____

Anger

_____

Self-centeredness

_____

4. Select two or three of the following "divine resources" and explain why they are important in dealing with depression: prayer, forgiveness, confession of sin, obedience, acceptance, yielding "rights," the body of Christ, God's grace, the Word, praise, and faith.

_____
_____
_____

5. What are some "natural" or human resources God provides that could be helpful in dealing with depression? (For example, nutritious food, sunlight, medical treatment . . .)

_____
_____

6. Many Christians have experienced a "dark night of the soul" even while they are walking with God. Read Isaiah 50:10, Hebrews 4:14–16, and 12:3. According to God's Word, what should a believer do at such times?

_____

_____

## RESPOND

7. Someone suffering with depression may feel that God is very far away or nonexistent. The psalmist was often tempted to feel this way (see Psalm 42:10). How did the writer of Psalm 42 handle this feeling of being "cast down"? Write Psalm 42:11 in your own words below, putting your name where the psalmist says "O my soul." Write this verse on a card and put it in a place where you will be reminded to quote it to yourself as needed.

_____

_____

> NOTE FROM *Nancy*
>
> *"At some level, illness (whether physical, emotional, or mental), pain, and depression are an unavoidable consequence of living in a fallen world. As the apostle Paul reminds us in Romans 8, the entire creation 'groans' under the weight of its sinful condition, longing for our final redemption."* (pp. 242–43)

*Lord, You are my Light in the darkness, my Hope in times of despair, and my Helper in life's most desperate hours. You lift up my head. No matter how great the darkness I am experiencing emotionally, help me to look to You, to wait patiently for You, and to trust that You are faithful and that Your mercy and grace will sustain me. Amen.*

## WALKING TOGETHER IN THE TRUTH . . .

1. In your reading and study of chapter 9, what Truth(s) did you find especially encouraging or helpful? (See pages 252–53 in *Lies Women Believe*.) Did you find any of these Truths difficult to accept?

_____

_____

■ **LIE #37: If I feel something, it must be true.**

■ **TRUTH:** Our feelings cannot always be trusted. They often have little to do with reality and can easily deceive us into believing things that are not true. We must choose to reject any feelings that are not consistent with the Truth.

2.  Describe a time when your emotions were misleading and didn't match what was really true in a situation. Did you choose to believe your feelings, or did you reject your feelings and believe the Truth? What was the result?

    _____

    _____

- **LIE #38: I can't control my emotions.**
- **TRUTH:** We do not have to be controlled by our emotions. We can choose to fix our minds on the Truth, to take every thought captive to the Truth, and to let God control our emotions.

3.  Read 2 Corinthians 10:5. How can you truly "take every thought captive to obey Christ"? What difference will that make in your life?

    _____

    _____

NOTE FROM *Nancy*

*"We have a Savior who cares deeply about those who suffer. He is tender and compassionate toward those who are weak and struggling. . . . And Scripture urges us to show the same compassion toward hurting people."* (p. 249)

- **LIE #39: I can't help how I respond when my hormones are out of whack.**
- **TRUTH:** By God's grace, we can choose to obey Him regardless of how we feel. There is no excuse for ungodly attitudes, responses, or behavior. Our physical and emotional cycles and seasons are under the control of the One who made us, cares for us, and has made provision for each stage of our lives.

4.  Hormonal changes are very real—no woman will contest that. What provision(s) has God made to help us deal with those changes in a way that glorifies Him?

    _____

    _____

5.  In what ways can the fluctuating emotions that may accompany our monthly cycle, pregnancy, or menopause actually draw us closer to the Lord?

    _____

    _____

- **LIE #40: I can't bear being depressed.**
- **TRUTH:** Physical and emotional symptoms of depression are sometimes the fruit of issues in the spirit that need to be addressed. Regardless of how we feel, we can choose to give thanks, to obey God, and to reach out to others. God has given us powerful resources—His grace, His Spirit, His Word, His promises, the body of Christ—to minister to our emotional needs.

6. Can you think of any reasons why depression may have become so widespread among women in the Western Hemisphere?

   _____

   _____

7. What are some of the heart issues that can cause physical or emotional symptoms of depression? Why is it important to deal with those issues?

   _____

   _____

8. What are some of the resources (natural and supernatural) God has made available that can minister grace to a woman suffering from depression?

   _____

   _____

   _____

9. Read together Lamentations 3:1–33. Describe the anguish Jeremiah felt. In what did Jeremiah ultimately place his hope?

   _____

   _____

   _____

10. Encourage a few women in your group to share how they have experienced the truth of Lamentations 3:21–26 in their walk with God.

NOTE FROM *Nancy*

*"We must remember that 'feeling good' is not the ultimate objective in the Christian's life. . . . As long as we are in these bodies, we will experience varying degrees of pain and distress. . . . The focus of our lives must not be so much on changing or 'fixing' things to make ourselves feel better as on the glory of God and His redemptive purposes in the world. . . . True joy comes from abandoning ourselves to that end." (p. 251)*

CHAPTER TEN

# DEALING WITH *Circumstances*

## IN A NUTSHELL . . .

Chapter 10 applies to every one of us, for we all have "circumstances." Our situations in life are as varied as the people involved. And how we react to our circumstances—whether we believe the lies presented to us by Satan or embrace God's Truth—has a profound effect on everything else. Some circumstances, of course, are beyond our control. If we fail to see the sovereign hand of God behind them, what comes into our lives will be vulnerable to confusion, frustration, bitterness, anger, and despair.

One lie we are tempted to believe is that if only our circumstances were different, then *we* would be different—we would act differently or we would be happier. What we are really saying is that we are victims of our circumstances. The Truth is, our circumstances do not make us what we are; they merely reveal what we are. We may not be able to control our circumstances, but by God's grace we can choose how we respond to them.

Another way many believers have been deceived is by the idea that they shouldn't have to suffer. But Jesus never promised an easy life. In fact, the Scriptures teach that it is impossible to become like Jesus—to be holy—apart from suffering. If we don't understand the necessity and value of suffering, we will be more concerned about getting relief from our pain than about discovering the pure fruit God wants to produce in our lives *through* the pain.

Yet another lie we may fall for is that our circumstances will never change. If we believe this lie, we will grow discouraged and be tempted to give up when facing seemingly impossible circumstances. In order to walk in freedom, we must exchange our temporal, earthly perspective for a heavenly one. Even if nothing changes in our lifetime, the years we experience on this earth are a mere blip on the timeline of eternity. So we can pray for God to intervene, but we must be patient when He does not act as quickly as we'd like. We must trust, obey, hope, and persevere even as we await God's answers. And we must keep our eyes fixed on Christ and the eternal joy awaiting us in heaven!

The fourth lie—"I just can't take any more!"—deceives many people into simply giving up when circumstances get hard. They believe that God has placed more on them than they can handle. But God promises that His grace is sufficient to help us in our weakness, no matter what circumstances may come our way.

The fifth lie, one we are all born believing, is pervasive in our society: "It's all about me." People who have fallen for this mindset feel and act as if nothing is more important than their own wants, needs, and desires. This attitude can easily lead to broken marriages, homes, and hearts. As believers, we are called to embrace the Truth that this life is all about God—not us. He is the reason we exist, and we should live to honor and glorify Him.

## EXPLORING THE TRUTH . . .

# ACCEPTING OUR CIRCUMSTANCES *(pp. 255–60)*
## DAY ONE

### REALIZE

1. Describe Eve's circumstances in the Garden before the entrance of sin. In spite of an ideal setting, Eve managed to become discontent and make a wrong choice. What does that say about our circumstances and our choices?

_____

_____

_____

### REFLECT

2. Look at the list of "if onlys" on pages 258–59 of *Lies Women Believe*. Do any of these apply to you? What are your personal "if onlys"—circumstances you tend to blame for your wrong responses or your lack of joy?

_____

_____

_____

NOTE FROM *Nancy*

*"We feel that if our circumstances were different—our upbringing, our environment, the people around us— we would be different. . . . The Truth is, our circumstances don't make us what we are. They merely reveal what we are." (p. 258)*

117

3. What sinful responses have you been excusing or rationalizing because of circumstances beyond your control (e.g., "I've not honored my husband, have spoken critically of him to others, and have been fretting because of his financial decisions")?

_____

_____

4. Give an example of a circumstance in your life that revealed something about your heart that needed to be changed (e.g., you became impatient while waiting in line at the supermarket).

_____

_____

5. Read 2 Corinthians 4:8–11, 16. How did the apostle Paul emerge from his circumstances as a victor rather than a victim?

_____

_____

## RESPOND

6. List one or more difficult circumstances you are facing at this time. Next to each circumstance, describe your inward and outward response to that situation. God may or may not choose to change your circumstance, but if you will let Him, He will use your circumstance to change you. What changes are needed in your attitude or your responses?

_____

_____

*Lord, I confess that I often let my circumstances control my attitudes and my responses.*
*I want to be controlled by Your Spirit. Please help me trust in You regardless of what is going on*
*around me, and teach me how to rejoice and be content in every circumstance. Amen.*

# PURPOSE IN SUFFERING *(pp. 260–62)*
## DAY TWO

### REALIZE

1. Why is suffering an inescapable fact of the human condition? Will we ever be totally free from suffering and pain while we live in this world? Why not?

_____

_____

_____

> ## NOTE FROM *Nancy*
>
> *"All the New Testament authors recognized that there is a redemptive, sanctifying fruit that cannot be produced in our lives except by suffering. In fact, Peter goes so far as to insist that suffering is our calling—not just for some select group of Christian leaders or martyrs, but for every child of God."* (p. 262)

2. Give one or two illustrations of the natural human instinct to avoid suffering.

_____

_____

_____

3. List several different kinds of suffering that you or others you know have had to endure (e.g., financial disaster, physical ailment, worry over a child).

_____

_____

### REFLECT

4. What do the following verses in the book of 1 Peter teach us about the purposes of God in suffering and how we should respond to suffering?

- 1:7

_____

- 2:21–23

_____

- 3:9

_____

- 3:14–17

- 4:1–2

- 4:12–16, 19

- 5:8–10

5. The suffering you have experienced thus far in your life may seem insignificant compared to what we read about in 1 Peter. But God can use every type of inconvenience or suffering in a redemptive, sanctifying way in our lives. Give an illustration of good or godly fruit that suffering has produced in your life.

## RESPOND

6. How could a painful situation you are facing at this time be for you "a pathway to sanctification and a doorway into greater intimacy with God" (*Lies Women Believe*, page 261)?

*Father, thank You that You use suffering to make us more like Your Son, who suffered for us.
I don't want to forfeit the blessings You can bring to me and to others through my pain.
Help me to embrace suffering when it comes and to allow You to fulfill all Your purposes
in and through my life. Amen.*

# GAINING AN ETERNAL PERSPECTIVE *(pp. 263–65)*
## DAY THREE

## REALIZE

1. What do we learn from the following Bible characters?

   - God promised to end Sarah's barrenness and give her and Abraham a child. How long did they wait for that promise to come true? (Genesis 12:4–5; 21:5)

   _____

   - How long was Joseph in prison—for a crime he didn't commit—after the cupbearer promised to bring Joseph's case to Pharaoh? (Genesis 40:23—41:1)

   _____

   - Joshua prayed for victory over his enemies. How quickly did God answer his request? (Joshua 10:12–14)

   _____

   - Mary and Martha knew that Jesus could heal their sick brother, Lazarus. How long did they wait before Jesus returned to them? (John 11:17)

   _____

> NOTE FROM *Nancy*
>
> *"Your night of weeping may go on for months or even years. But if you are a child of God, it will not go on forever. God has determined the exact duration of your suffering, and it will not last one moment longer than He knows is necessary to achieve His holy, eternal purposes in and through your life."*
> *(p. 264)*

2. Describe a time when you prayed for something and it took a long time to get the response you were hoping for. (Or describe a prayer request for which you are still awaiting God's answer.)

   _____

## REFLECT

3. What purposes might God have for not solving a problem or changing a difficult circumstance as quickly as we wish? In what ways does God's waiting to answer our requests achieve His holy, eternal purposes in our lives?

   _____

   _____

4.According to Revelation 21:1–7, what do we have to look forward to? How can this vision help us endure pain and suffering in this life here on earth?

_____

_____

## RESPOND

5.  Read Psalm 130:5. Waiting is a deliberate action that often requires more courage than taking matters into our own hands. It requires trust, obedience, hope, and perseverance. What is one current situation in your life where you think you may need to simply, quietly wait on the Lord?

_____

_____

*Father, it can be hard to endure when it seems like nothing is changing in my circumstances.*
*Help me to wait for Your timing, knowing that You will act at the right time.*
*Until then, teach me to trust, obey, hope, and persevere. Be glorified in my life. Amen.*

# GOD'S GRACE IS SUFFICIENT *(pp. 265–67)*
## DAY FOUR

## REALIZE

1.  Why do you think many people choose to just give up—on their marriages, their jobs, their children?

_____

_____

2.  Describe a time when you were tempted to give up, throw in the towel, and say, "I just can't take any more." What caused you to feel that way? What did you do?

_____

_____

## REFLECT

3. Read 2 Corinthians 11:22–30. Do you think Paul ever felt like he just couldn't take any more? What do you think kept him going?

_____

_____

4. Now read 2 Corinthians 12:7–10. In what ways do you think Paul's "thorn in the flesh" was used by God? What did he learn about God's grace that he might not have learned any other way?

_____

_____

5. Is it sometimes wise *not* to continue in a certain activity, job, or situation? How can you know if you should hang on and persevere, or take steps to make a change?

_____

_____

_____

NOTE FROM *Nancy*

*"Dear child of God, your heavenly Father will never lead you anywhere that His grace will not carry you. When the path before you seems hopelessly long, take heart. Lift up your eyes. Look ahead to that day when all suffering will be over."* (p. 267)

## RESPOND

6. List two or three circumstances in your life that you cannot handle on your own. Then, write next to each circumstance: "Your grace is sufficient for me."

_____

_____

_____

_____

*Lord, sometimes I feel I simply can't take any more. I feel so very weak. Yet You promise that Your grace is sufficient for me and that Your strength is made perfect in my weakness. Help me to walk in Your grace and Your strength today. Thank You that by Your grace I can go on. Amen.*

# LIVING A GOD-CENTERED LIFE *(pp. 267–74)*
## DAY FIVE

### REALIZE

1. Why do you think you are alive? If you had to write a short life-purpose statement, what would you say?

_____

_____

### REFLECT

2. According to Revelation 4:11, why were we created?

_____

_____

3. Read Philippians 1:21–24 and 3:7–16. How would Paul answer the question, "Why are you alive?"

_____

_____

4. Read Acts 20:22–24. How did Paul's passion to fulfill God's purpose for his life enable him to endure and press on in following and serving Christ, in spite of adversity?

_____

_____

### RESPOND

5. What gets in the way of your being fully abandoned to Christ and His agenda in the world (e.g., particular people, goals, possessions, desires, etc.)?

_____

_____

6. Write a prayer confessing any areas of your life where you have been looking out primarily for yourself and your own interests. If you can honestly do so, express your desire to live a life that is wholly centered on God. If you're not quite there, ask God to change your heart and give you His desires and perspective.

_____

_____

_____

*Lord, I confess that my natural tendency is to look out for myself, my interests, and my happiness. But I realize that it's not about me—it's all about You and Your kingdom, Your will, Your glory. I was created to bring pleasure and glory to You. I know I will only find true joy as I lay down my life to that end. Amen.*

## WALKING TOGETHER IN THE TRUTH . . .

1. In your reading and study of chapter 10, what Truth did you find especially encouraging or helpful? (See pages 275–77 in *Lies Women Believe*.)

_____

_____

> NOTE FROM *Nancy*
>
> *"We've been deceived into believing we would be happier if we had a different set of circumstances. But the Truth is, if we're not content within our present circumstances, we're not likely to be happy in another set of circumstances." (p. 259)*

- **LIE #41: If my circumstances were different, I would be different.**
- **TRUTH:** Our circumstances do not make us what we are; they merely reveal what we are. If we're not content with our present circumstances, we're not likely to be happy in another set of circumstances. We may not be able to control our circumstances, but our circumstances don't have to control us. Every circumstance that touches our lives has first been filtered through God's fingers of love.

2. The apostle Paul faced constant problems and adversity. However, his circumstances never diminished his joy. In fact, he had this extraordinary testimony: "In all our affliction, I am overflowing with joy" (2 Corinthians 7:4). How could Paul experience real joy in the midst of tribulation? (For some clues, see 2 Corinthians 1:3–6 and Philippians 4:11–13.)

_____

_____

3. When faced with stressful circumstances, Elizabeth Prentiss wrote to her friend, "The experience of the past winter would impress upon me the fact that place and position have next to nothing to do with happiness; that we can be wretched in a palace, radiant in a dungeon"[3] (*Lies Women Believe*, p. 259). Do you agree with her? If so, why? How have you seen this insight illustrated in your own experience or someone else's?

_____

_____

■ **LIE #42: I shouldn't have to suffer.**

■ **TRUTH:** It's impossible to become like Jesus apart from suffering. There is redemptive fruit that cannot be produced in our lives apart from suffering. Suffering is a doorway into greater intimacy with God. True joy is not the absence of pain, but the presence of Christ in the midst of the pain.

### NOTE FROM *Nancy*

*"The Truth is, your pain—be it physical affliction, memories of abuse, a troubled marriage, or a heart broken by a wayward child—may go on for a long time. But it will not last forever. It may go on for all of your life down here on this earth. But even a lifetime is not forever."*
(p. 263)

4. What blessings or benefits might we miss out on if we run from our suffering rather than embracing it and growing through it?

_____

_____

5. Share some of the insights you recorded from 1 Peter on pages 119–20 in this study guide. As you think about what you've learned about God's purposes in our suffering, how does that affect your perspective about a difficult situation you are currently facing?

_____

_____

■ **LIE #43: My circumstances will never change—this will go on forever.**

■ **TRUTH:** Our suffering may last a long time, but it will not last forever. Our painful circumstances will not last one moment longer than God knows is necessary to achieve His eternal purposes in and through our lives. One day all pain, suffering, and tears will be removed forever.

6. Read James 1:2–4. What is the connection between trials and spiritual maturity? Why is it important for believers to learn perseverance, and how is it developed?

_____

_____

---

3. George Lewis Prentiss, ed., *More Love to Thee: The Life and Letters of Elizabeth Prentiss* (Amityville, NY: Calvary, 1994), 374.

7. Read Romans 8:18 and 2 Corinthians 4:17–18. What hope do these verses give us? How does looking ahead help us face trials that seem to go on and on?

_____

_____

- **LIE #44: I just can't take any more.**
- **TRUTH:** Whatever our circumstance, whatever our situation, His grace is sufficient for us. God will never place more on us than He will give us grace to bear.

8. Ask two or three women in your group to share a brief example of how they found God's grace to be sufficient when they were facing a situation where they felt they just couldn't go on.

_____

_____

> ### NOTE FROM *Nancy*
>
> *"Whether we choose to believe it or not, if we are God's children, the Truth is that His grace really is sufficient for us. . . . His grace is sufficient for every moment, every circumstance, every detail, every need, and every failure of our lives."*
> (p. 266)

9. An important way we can minister to one another in the body of Christ is to remind each other that the grace of God truly is sufficient for all our needs and to encourage each other to exercise faith in His provision.

   Ask any in your group who wish to do so to share in one sentence a circumstance she is currently facing that seems unbearable at times (for example, a child addicted to drugs, a pressing deadline at work, etc.). As each need is expressed, have the whole group respond aloud together, "His grace is sufficient for you." Then, have the woman who shared respond back to the group, "His grace is sufficient for me." Then move on and let another share a situation for which she needs God's grace, responding in the same way for each individual. (Don't whisper your responses—say with conviction, "His grace is sufficient!")

- **LIE #45: It's all about me.**
- **TRUTH:** God is the beginning and ending and center of all things. All things were created by Him and for Him. Our lives are dispensable. We were created for His pleasure and glory.

10. What does it mean to live "coram Deo" (see page 270 in *Lies Women Believe*)? What difference would it make in our world if Christian women lived this way? How would your life look different if you were to live each day this way?

_____

_____

_____

_____

# CHAPTER ELEVEN

# WALKING IN *Freedom*

## IN A NUTSHELL...

Chapters 11 and 12 conclude the book with advice about how to counter Satan's lies with God's Truth. The entire book is structured around these two related concepts:

- Believing lies places us in bondage
- The Truth has the power to set us free

Some of us may need to address areas of deeply entrenched deception. We all need to be alert and on guard for Satan's lies and take him seriously. God's Word reminds us: "Your adversary the devil prowls around like a roaring lion, seeking someone to devour" (1 Peter 5:8). His methods are cunning and deceptive. Knowing that we may not readily fall for outright lies, he feeds us subtle propaganda. Judging from the bondage that many women live in, he is doing a pretty good job of selling his subtle lies and half-truths. It's easy to see the consequences of his deception all around us.

The good news is that the Truth is always stronger than any lie, just as our Savior is always stronger than our Enemy. Believers are not immune to Satan's attacks, but we do have weapons to protect us from them—the absolute Truth of God's Word, the redeeming love and grace of Christ, and the power of the indwelling Holy Spirit.

God's Truth has the power to help us discern Satan's lies and then to set us free, as we appropriate His grace in our daily lives. Every time we hear a message, regardless of its source, we should evaluate it in the light of His Word. The better acquainted we are with the Word, the better equipped we will be to identify Satan's lies and counter them with God's Truth.

When we learn the Truth, believe it, surrender to it, and live it out by His grace, we will be freed to experience the abundant life Christ came to give us, and we can help point others to the Truth that will set them free.

**EXPLORING THE TRUTH . . .**

# SURRENDERING TO THE TRUTH *(pp. 279–88)*
## DAY ONE

### REALIZE

1. Look through the lies listed in the table of contents for *Lies Women Believe*. During the course of this study, has the Lord shown you any specific areas where you have been deceived? List one or more lies (either from the list in *Lies Women Believe* or others that you have identified) that you now realize you have fallen for.

_____

_____

_____

2. Describe how believing those lies has put you in bondage.

_____

_____

### REFLECT

3. What corresponding Truth from God's Word counters each lie you listed above? Write the Truth(s) below and note where you can find them in the Bible. (You'll find a list of corresponding lies and Truths, along with related Scriptures, at the end of each chapter in *Lies*.)

_____

_____

_____

4. How can the Truths you have identified set you free from bondage and make you more like Jesus?

_____

_____

_____

NOTE FROM *Nancy*

*"The Truth has the power to overcome every lie. This is what the Enemy doesn't want you to realize. As long as you believe his lies, he can keep you in bondage. But once you know the Truth and start believing and acting on it, the prison doors will swing open and you will be set free."* (p. 282)

## RESPOND

5. Just knowing the Truth is not enough. We must surrender ourselves to the Truth. What do you need to change in your thinking or your lifestyle that is not in line with the Truth of God's Word?

_____

_____

*Lord, thank You for showing me the lies that have held me in bondage and the Truth that can set me free. Please help me to believe and act on the Truth every time a lie presents itself. Amen.*

# WALKING IN THE TRUTH ABOUT GOD *(pp. 289–91)*

## DAY TWO

### TRUTHS 1–6

## REALIZE

1. Review each of the first six Truths in the list that begins on page 290. Then look up the corresponding verses and describe how the verses affirm the Truth.

Truth #1: Psalm 119:68; 136:1

_____

_____

Truth #2: Romans 8:32, 38–39

_____

_____

Truth #3: Ephesians 1:4–6

_____

_____

Truth #4: Psalm 23:1

_____

_____

Truth #5: Isaiah 26:3–4

_____

_____

_____

Truth #6: Isaiah 46:10

_____

_____

_____

> NOTE FROM *Nancy*
>
> *"Each time the Enemy bombards us with lies, we must learn to counsel our hearts according to the Truth and to act on the Truth, regardless of what our human reason or our feelings tell us."*
> (p. 282)

## REFLECT

2. Choose a Truth from the list above that you feel you most need to hold on to today. Write it below.

_____

_____

## RESPOND

3. List one or two concrete changes you will make, with God's help, to act on the Truth you just chose. Then pray the prayer below, inserting the Truth and the changes you chose into the blanks.

_____

_____

> *Lord, thank You for Your Word that tells me the Truth about who You are,*
> *what You have done for me, and how much You love me.*
> *I receive the Truth that* _____ ,
> *and I will act on that Truth today by* _____ . *Amen.*

# WALKING IN THE TRUTH OF
# CHRIST'S SUFFICIENCY *(pp. 292–94)*

## DAY THREE

### TRUTHS 7–11

## REALIZE

1. Review the next five Truths in the list—beginning with #7 on page 292. Then look up the corresponding verses and describe how the verses affirm the Truth.

   Truth #7: 2 Corinthians 12:9

   _____

   _____

   Truth #8: 1 John 1:7

   _____

   _____

   Truth #9: Romans 6:6–7

   _____

   _____

   Truth #10: 1 Corinthians 6:9–11

   _____

   _____

   Truth #11: Psalm 19:7; 107:20; 119:105

   _____

   _____

## REFLECT

2. Choose a Truth from the list above that you feel you most need to hold on to today. Write it below.

   _____

   _____

## RESPOND

3. List one or two concrete changes you will make, with God's help, to act on the Truth you just chose. Then pray the prayer below, inserting the Truth and the changes you chose into the blanks.

_____

_____

*Lord, thank You that Your grace is sufficient to help me even in my deepest need or strongest bondage. I receive the Truth that _____, and I will act on that Truth today by _____. Amen.*

# WALKING IN THE TRUTH BY
# RELINQUISHING CONTROL *(pp. 294–96)*
## DAY FOUR

### TRUTHS 12–17

## REALIZE

1. Review each of the next six Truths in the list, beginning on page 294. Then look up the corresponding verses and describe how the verses affirm the Truth.

Truth #12: 1 Thessalonians 5:24; Philippians 2:13

_____

_____

Truth #13: Ezekiel 18:19–22

_____

_____

Truth #14: Galatians 6:7–8

_____

_____

Truth #15: Matthew 16:25; Luke 1:38; 1 Peter 5:7

_____

_____

Truth #16: Romans 13:1; 1 Peter 3:1–6

_____

_____

Truth #17: Ephesians 5:26–27

_____

_____

## REFLECT

2. Choose a Truth from the list above that you feel you most need to hold on to today. Write it below.

_____

_____

## RESPOND

3. List one or two concrete changes you will make, with God's help, to act on the Truth you just chose. Then pray the prayer below, inserting the Truth and the changes you chose into the blanks.

_____

_____

*Lord, thank You that I can find joy and freedom by relinquishing control of my life to You.*
*I understand that true freedom is found by submitting to You.*
*I receive the Truth that _____ ,*
*and I will act on that Truth today by _____. Amen.*

# WALKING IN THE TRUTH BY GLORIFYING GOD *(pp. 297–302)*

## DAY FIVE

### TRUTHS 18-21

### REALIZE

1. Review each of the final four Truths, beginning on page 297. Then look up the corresponding verses and describe how the verses affirm the Truth.

Truth #18: Romans 8:29

_____

_____

_____

Truth #19: 1 Peter 5:10

_____

_____

_____

Truth #20: 2 Corinthians 4:17–18

_____

_____

_____

Truth #21: Colossians 1:16–18; Revelation 4:11

_____

_____

_____

### REFLECT

2. Choose a Truth from the list above that you feel you most need to hang on to today. Write it below.

_____

_____

> NOTE FROM *Nancy*
>
> *"Once we agree with God that we exist for His pleasure and His glory, we can accept whatever comes into our lives as part of His sovereign will and purpose. We will not resent or resist the hard things, but embrace them as friends, sovereignly designed by God to make us like Jesus and to bring glory to Himself. We will be able to look into His face and say, 'It's not about me. It's about You. If it pleases You, it pleases me. All that matters is that You are glorified.'"* (p. 299)

## RESPOND

3. List one or two specific changes you will make, with God's help, to act on the Truth you just chose. Then pray the prayer below, inserting the Truth and the changes you chose into the blanks.

_____

_____

*Lord, thank You that this life is a whole lot bigger than just me.*
*You have put me on this earth to glorify You and bring You pleasure.*
*That is what I want to do, Lord, today and every day of my life.*
*As I do, You have promised that I will experience fullness of joy and the delights of Your pleasures.*
*I receive the Truth that* _____ *,*
*and I will act on that Truth today by* _____ *. Amen.*

# WALKING TOGETHER IN THE TRUTH . . .

1. Read the Epilogue in *Lies Women Believe* (pp. 301–302) together. How did Eve experience God's mercy and grace after the fall? How does that give you hope?

_____

_____

2. What resources has God made available to protect us from deception? What are some practical ways we can guard our minds and hearts?

_____

_____

3. What have you learned in this study about Satan's lies and God's Truth that was new to you or that you needed to be reminded of?

_____

_____

4. How has your thinking changed as a result of this study?

_____

_____

5. Can you share a specific illustration of how the Truth has begun to change your life and set you free since you started this study?

_____

_____

6. It's not always easy to walk in the Truth and proclaim it to others. To do so requires that we swim upstream against the flow of our culture—and sometimes even against the flow of "Christian culture." List some biblical Truths that fly in the face of our culture.

_____

_____

_____

NOTE FROM *Nancy*

*"In Christ and in His Word, we have the Truth that sets people free. That is Good News! And there is no other way for those we know and love to be delivered from darkness, deception, and death. . . . Let's learn the Truth, believe it, surrender to it, and live it out. . . . Then let's proclaim the Truth with boldness, conviction, and compassion, seeking to bring wandering brothers and sisters back to Christ." (p. 288)*

7. Why is it so important for believers to walk according to the Truth and to seek to point others to the Truth?

_____

_____

_____

8. Share an illustration of how God used another individual to restore you when you were blind to the Truth or had wandered away from it.

_____

_____

_____

9. Close your time together with prayer, thanking God for the riches and greatness of His Truth, freshly surrendering yourselves to live for His pleasure and glory and asking Him to use each woman in your group to point others to the Truth that can set them free.

# SUGGESTIONS FOR
## GROUP *Leaders*

*T*hank you for being willing to facilitate a group study of *Lies Women Believe*! If this is a new role for you, you may be wondering how to begin. The following suggestions are meant to provide some practical tips for leading this study. I pray God will give you wisdom to help the women in your group grasp the importance of grounding their lives in the Truth of Christ and His Word.

This study is a companion to my book *Lies Women Believe* (updated and expanded, 2018), which addresses some common falsehoods that many Christian women have come to accept. Some of these lies are obviously untrue but have been unconsciously internalized by many women, absorbed from the surrounding culture. Others are more subtle or are half-truths, making them more difficult to identify. But whether the lies are overt or subtle, when we believe them, we ultimately end up in bondage.

My desire is to see women identify the lies that have ensnared them and then counter those lies with the Truth that can set them free. This study is designed to help women go further in that process through an eleven-week journey that includes personal study and application and, ideally, a weekly gathering where women can interact with each other on these important topics.

### DISCUSSING THE TRUTH—HANDLING DIFFERENCES

The first purpose of the weekly group session is to provide an opportunity for women to discuss the material presented in each chapter and to develop greater understanding of the Truth.

As you talk through the questions each week, remember that the goal is not to deal exhaustively with any of the specific topics, but to help women get a broad overview of the major theme of the chapter. Resist the temptation to give too much time to a single lie. And encourage the women to keep their answers brief so as many women as possible can participate.

You may find that there is disagreement within your group on one or more particular topics. I understand that some sincere believers may not share some of my positions. Allow for open, honest discussion. However, encourage the women to express their differences in a spirit of humility and without being argumentative or divisive (see Titus 3:2).

Let the women know on the front end that you don't want to bog down on individual points where there may be differences. Explain how important it is that they base their responses on the Word of God and not on their personal opinions or what they may have always assumed to be true.

The ultimate goal of the study is not to get women to agree with you or me on every point, but to get them to search out the Scripture for themselves so they can learn to discern Satan's lies and to know and obey the Truth.

## APPLYING THE TRUTH—ENCOURAGING PARTICIPATION

The second purpose of the group session is to provide an opportunity for women to open their hearts to each other, to share how they have been living out the Truth they have been learning, and to encourage each other in their walk with God. Explain from the outset that any personal sharing is to be treated as confidential and should not be taken outside the group (unless something is said that requires legal or pastoral intervention).

Depending on the nature and extent of the lies that have been embraced, this study may surface painful issues in some women's hearts. Ask the Lord to show you how to come alongside these women to help them find freedom in the Truth and to point them to the God of all grace, comfort, and peace.

If the women in your group don't know each other well or are not accustomed to sharing on a personal level, they may be more reserved at first. Don't get discouraged. As they get more comfortable with each other, they will likely feel more free to open up.

At times, you may need to direct the conversation so the time isn't dominated by one or a few women. If you sense someone is struggling, rather than letting her need consume the group's time together, you may want to set up a time for the two of you to talk together. You may also want to offer to meet privately with a participant who seems to need extra time. You don't want the group time to turn into a therapy session. Ask the Lord to give you sensitivity and wisdom as you steer the discussion.

Allow the Holy Spirit to work with each woman individually. Some women may be quick to identify issues that need to be addressed in their lives. Others may recognize that they have believed a lie, but may need time for God to show them what changes to make or to find the courage to make those changes. Still others may resist identifying lies they have believed. Be patient with each person. Trust God to work in each life in His way and His time.

## PREPARATION FOR GROUP SESSIONS

As a leader, you'll want to do the study along with your group. However, if possible, read through *Lies Women Believe* ahead of time so you understand the big picture.

Make sure each member of your group has her own copy of a Bible, *Lies Women Believe* (the 2018 version), and this Study Guide. Encourage participants to complete the lessons for Days One through Five in each chapter prior to the group meeting. (They don't need to complete the "Walking Together in the Truth" section as those questions will be covered during your group discussion.)

Group members will get more out of the study if they work through the lessons on their own. However, some women may find it difficult to complete all the homework each week. Encourage them to at least read the chapter from *Lies* before the group session. It's more important that they hear the Truth than that they answer every question.

## STRUCTURE AND FORMAT

Assuming there are at least several women in your group, an ideal time frame for the group session is two hours. Here is a suggested schedule if you have that much time available:

| | |
|---|---|
| 10 minutes | Fellowship (perhaps with light refreshments) |
| 5 minutes | Welcome and opening prayer |
| 5 minutes | Read "In a Nutshell" |
| 90 minutes | Group discussion and interaction |
| 10 minutes | Prayer time |

If you are using this study in a setting where your time is more limited, you can adjust accordingly.

Begin your time together with prayer, asking the Lord for wisdom and guidance in your discussion. Then have someone(s) read aloud the "In a Nutshell" section, which is a brief overview of the chapter. This will help refresh everyone's memory as well as include those who may not have finished their homework.

The group discussion is intended to be an overview of the topic with a few questions devoted to each lie and the corresponding Truth. Depending on how much time you have and how interactive your group is, feel free to pick and choose certain questions to discuss together. Some weeks you may cover all the questions; other weeks your group may discuss fewer questions.

Close your group time in prayer for one another. You can pray as a group or divide into pairs or smaller groups if that works better in your situation.

## SEEKING GOD FOR CHANGE

Pray for each session and for each member of your group. Ask God to open the women's eyes and hearts to whatever He may want to teach them through the course of this study. Don't make assumptions about the women in your group. The woman who appears the most put together on the outside may be struggling in ways others can't see. The quietest one may have great depth. The most outgoing one may have the most needs—or vice versa. Ask God to give you discernment so you can minister effectively to each woman.

If a group member is dealing with a complex or difficult issue, you may want to suggest that she seek further help from her pastor or another spiritual leader in her church. Continue to offer God's Truth and encouragement, and pray that God will help you lead the women to His throne, where they can receive mercy and grace to meet their need (see Hebrews 4:16).

God promises that if we seek Him with all our hearts, we will find Him. His Truth is the greatest power for change in the universe. Expect to see lives changed through this study—including your own. I pray you will experience His presence, His grace, and His Truth in a powerful way as you lead this group. May Christ be magnified through your efforts!

# THANK YOU!

Many hearts and hands have joined together to help produce this Study Guide. Special thanks to the following fellow-servants whose behind-the-scenes labors have not gone unnoticed and will be more fully rewarded in That Day:

- The *Moody Publishers* team—Randall Payleitner, Judy Dunagan, Erik Peterson, and Connor Sterchi—each with your areas of expertise and your eagerness to serve—all the way to the finish line.

- *Erin Davis* and *Anne Buchanan* for your editorial efforts on a project that turned out to be a lot bigger than any of us anticipated.

- *Erik Wolgemuth, Mike Neises, Sandy Bixel*, and *Hannah Kurtz* for running interference and providing assistance on various administrative fronts.

- *Logan Mroczek*, who keeps my laptop going and more than once (including nights and weekends on occasion) has kept me from losing my sanity and my sanctification, when I was panicking due to some wonky formatting issue, a manuscript vanishing from my screen, or a foreboding notice appearing in its place.

- My DH (*dear husband*), *Robert Wolgemuth*, whose companionship, love, encouragement, and prayers bring joy to my heart and help to lighten my load each day.

May Christ continue to bless and anoint your labors and be magnified through this resource.

# I'D LOVE TO HEAR FROM YOU

Dear friend,

What a privilege it has been to walk with you through this journey as we have plumbed our hearts and explored the Truth of God's Word together.

If this study has been meaningful or helpful to you, would you take a few moments to share how God has used it in your life? Go to liesbooks.com/contact, where you'll find a few questions to help prime the pump. Thanks so much for taking time to share your story. It will be a great encouragement to me and to the team at *Revive Our Hearts*.

*Revive Our Hearts* exists to help women experience freedom, fullness, and fruitfulness in Christ. To learn more about the various resources we have available, or to let us know how we can serve you or the women in your church, contact us at:

ReviveOurHearts.com
P.O. Box 2000 • Niles, MI 49120

May you continue to experience the freedom and joy of walking in the Truth! And may He use you as an instrument of grace and Truth in the lives of others around you.

Every blessing to you in Christ,

Nancy

Nancy DeMoss Wolgemuth